Practise and Pass
B1 Preliminary
for Schools

Student's Book

Megan Roderick
Bernardo Morales

 Access all the accompanying digital components for this book on **allango**, the DELTA Publishing language learning platform:

 Scan the QR code or go directly to **www.allango.co.uk** | Search for the title or the ISBN and click on the cover image | Access content, use now or save for later

 When you see this symbol, accompanying digital content is available.

DELTA Publishing

1st edition   3 | 2025

The last figure shown denotes the year of impression.

All rights reserved. No part of this publication may be reproduced, stored in a retrieval system, or transmitted, in any form or by any means, electronic, mechanical, photocopying, recording, or otherwise, without prior written permission from the publisher.

Delta Publishing, 2020

www.deltapublishing.co.uk

www.klett-sprachen.de/delta

© Ernst Klett Sprachen GmbH, Rotebühlstraße 77, D-70178 Stuttgart, 2020
Use of the content for text and data mining is expressly reserved and therefore prohibited.

Author: Megan Roderick, Bernardo Morales
Editor: Kate Baade
Layout and typesetting: Greta Gröttrup
Illustrations: Greta Gröttrup, Alek Sotirovski
Cover: Andreas Drabarek
Cover picture: Shutterstock (Panthep Boonsaree), New York;
Printing and binding: Elanders Waiblingen GmbH, Waiblingen

Printed in Germany
ISBN 978-3-12-501703-0

CONTENTS

Preparation Path	4
Prepare for B1 Preliminary	6
Reading Part 1	10
Reading Part 2	16
Reading Part 3	22
Reading Part 4	28
Reading Part 5	34
Reading Part 6	40
Reading: Perfect!	46
Writing Part 1	48
Writing Part 2	54
Writing: Perfect!	60
Listening Part 1	62
Listening Part 2	68
Listening Part 3	74
Listening Part 4	80
Listening: Perfect!	86
Speaking Part 1	88
Speaking Part 2	94
Speaking Part 3	100
Speaking Part 4	106
Speaking: Perfect!	112
Practice Test	114
Preparation Pack	132

Preparation Path

PREPARE

Exam Paper	Part	Unit	Focus on language
Reading	1	Do you get the message?	Communication
	2	What's on this weekend?	Entertainment and media
	3	What's your favourite place?	Places
	4	How do you stay healthy?	Hobbies and leisure; food and drink
	5	How do you like to travel?	Travel and transport; clothes and accessories
	6	How digital are you?	Technology and education
Writing	1	What can we do to help the environment?	Environment, weather, nature
	2	How fit and healthy are you?	Health, medicine and exercise
Listening	1	How do you help out at home?	House and home; shopping for groceries
	2	How are you feeling?	Personal feelings; opinions and agreement
	3	How great is this town?	Places: town and city; services
	4	What do you want to do later?	Work and jobs
Speaking	1	Can you tell me about yourself?	All about you
	2	What can you see?	Describing pictures
	3	What should we do?	Making suggestions, discussing alternatives and making decisions
	4	What do you like doing?	Opinions and preferences
Extra Resources			Preparation Pack

PRACTISE AND PASS

Focus on the exam task → Do the exam task

- Read five short messages and choose between three options.
- Read about five people and eight different situations. Match each person to the correct tense.
- Read a long text with five multiple-choice questions.
- Find the five correct missing sentences from a text.
- Read a text with six missing words. Answer six multiple-choice questions and choose the correct word.
- Complete six gaps in a text with one word of your own choice.
- Read an email with four notes attached and write a reply.
- Write a story or an article. (100 words)
- Listen to seven short audio recordings and choose the correct image.
- Listen to six short dialogues and choose the right answer.
- Listen to a long text and complete the gaps with missing information.
- Listen to a long text and answer six questions about the meaning, attitudes and opinions.
- Answer the examiner's general social questions.
- Describe a photograph.
- Work together with the other candidate(s) to complete a task.
- Following on from the topic in Speaking 3, talk about your preferences and opinions.

Practice Test
Additional online Practice Test

PERFECT!

Perform even better!

- ☑ **Exam tips**
- ☑ **Exam paper and process familiarisation**
- ☑ **Preparation Pack**
- ☑ **Practice Tests**
- ☑ **PERFECT! sections at the end of each Exam Paper type.**

Prepare for B1 Preliminary

What to expect

Match Javi's question with the teacher's answer.

1 What does B1 mean?

a It means you can understand and use phrases and expressions so that you can understand things like instructions, articles you find online or in magazines, factual information at school. You can also join in in most conversations and talk about every day topics. As far as writing is concerned, you can write emails, messages and letters, and you can express your opinion on a lot of topics.

2 Do I have to go to an exam centre to take the exam?

b Your ability to use and understand vocabulary, grammar and phrases that the examiner expects you to be familiar with at level B1. You can find out more specific information by searching for B1 Preliminary on the internet.

3 How will I get my exam results?

c Yes, there are lots of things you can do to prepare. The aim of this book is to help you get ready to pass! As well as the activities we'll work through, there are additional resources at the back with vocabulary, grammar and phrases that will help you express yourself at a B1 level.

4 What will I be tested on?

d Don't worry about that, all examiners are trained to manage situations like this and make sure that you get a chance to speak and interact.

5 In the Speaking Paper there will be another candidate. What if they speak too much and I don't get a chance?

e Practise as much as you can. And try to remember that the examiner just wants to hear you speak and mistakes are normal. If you can relax, then the Speaking exam can actually be fun!

6 What happens if I fail this exam?

f For the paper-based exam, yes. Some centres work with the computer-based exam. You'll need to contact your centre to find out.

Right now, I feel _____

_____

_____ about taking the B1 Preliminary exam.

Prepare

Prepare for B1 Preliminary

7 Can I do anything to prepare?

g You will either receive a Pass with Merit or a Pass if you did well enough. If you didn't manage to score high enough, the Candidate Profile you receive will show you how you did in all the papers, so that you can improve your performance next time. You will need to learn a bit more before trying again! A really good place to start is with the Cambridge B1 Vocabulary List.

8 I get really nervous when I'm speaking. What can I do about this?

h You'll get a certificate with a score for each paper and an overall score. Your grade and CEFR level are based on your overall score.

The exam structure

1 Look through the book and in the internet. Complete the sentences with a number from the box. You can use the numbers here more than once.

| 11 | 30 | 12 | 6 | 15 | 2 | 3 | 45 | 32 | 25 | 4 | 100 |

1 In the exam there are _____ papers.

2 The Reading paper has _____ parts. You have _____ minutes to complete this paper.

3 You have _____ minutes to complete the Writing paper. There are _____ parts. The message email and article or story you write must be about _____ words long.

4 The Listening paper takes _____ minutes, and the Speaking paper is only about _____ minutes, or _____ if there are _____ candidates in the room.

5 Most students who use this book are aged between _____ and _____.

6 There are _____ questions in the Reading paper.

7 There are _____ questions in the Listening paper.

8 There are at least _____ candidates in the room during the Speaking paper. There are always _____ examiners.

9 The total length of the exam is approximately _____ hours and _____ minutes.

I now know a bit about the exam. This is how I'm going to find out more: _____

_____

Practise

7

Prepare for B1 Preliminary

On the day

1 Before the exam you have to… Look at the advice and put the sentences in the correct order.

1 on arrive time
_____

2 an you take a make and sure you pencil eraser with
_____

3 your phone your put in bag
_____

4 examiner show the identification some
_____

2 During the exam you have to… Read these sentences and decide if they are true (T) or false (F).

1 Write all your answers on the sheet. T☐ F☐

2 You need to complete the answer sheet with a pen. T☐ F☐

3 You can have five minutes to finish writing after the examiner has said you must stop. T☐ F☐

4 Keep your eye on the clock and make sure you have enough time for all parts. T☐ F☐

> **IN THIS BOOK…**
> - Each unit starts with a "What you have to do" box. This tells you clearly what the task in the paper is.
> - Each Pass! Section includes Paper specific exam tips.
> - Perfect! sections after each paper consolidate key advice.

3 At the end of a task or a paper you should / have to… Fill in the gap with exam–related words starting with the letter given.

Always __c_____ that you have answered the __q_____ and that you did exactly what the __i_____ say. Allow some __t____ to read what you have written. In the Listening papers, make sure you didn't leave any answers __b____ and make sure you __t_____ your answers to the __a____ __s_____ correctly. __R____ your hand if you need help.

4 Write as many words as you can remember connected with exams in this box.

instructions   transfer

Learning more words is really important. This is how I'm going to build my vocabulary: _____

Pass

8

Prepare for B1 Preliminary

Getting ready

1 Work in teams. How fast can you answer the questions?

How many papers are there in B1 Preliminary?

How many parts are there in total?

How long is the exam?

2 As a team write at least three more B1 Preliminary quiz questions. Ask the other teams the questions and answer their questions.

Your B1 Preliminary questions

3 Give your partner some advice about what they need to do to prepare for B1 Preliminary. They will also give you some advice. Make a note of the best piece of advice you received.

You should...

practise reading signs and messages.

do some timed exercises and exam tasks.

get better at working out the meaning of new words by looking at the words next to them in the text.

get a penfriend and write to them regularly.

I got some really great advice. The most important thing for me to focus on now is: _____

Perfect!

1 Reading

STEP 1 PREPARE

Do you get the message?

WHAT YOU HAVE TO DO

In this part:
- you have to read five short texts (emails, text messages, notices, announcements, etc).
- then you have to choose one of three options that means the same as what you have read in the text.

1 Look at the messages and notices in the photos. Where might you see them? What are some reasons for writing them?

2 Match opposite words and phrases from A and B. Then choose a suitable word or phrase to complete the sentences.

1	available ...	a	forbidden
2	decrease ...	b	increase
3	delayed ...	c	maximum
4	frequently ...	d	next
5	allowed ...	e	on time
6	minimum ...	f	out of stock
7	permanent ...	g	seldom
8	previous ...	h	temporary

1 My sister's job at the chemist's is only _____ – she'll be going back to college in September.

2 Fifty students is the _____ number that can travel on one coach.

3 Stephan plays tennis _____ with his father – that's why he's getting so good!

4 There's only one room _____ for the party so I hope that will be enough.

5 I'm sorry but those black boots are _____ at the moment. Can you try again next week?

6 It is _____ to play the drums or any loud musical instrument in the block of flats.

3 Replace the underlined parts of the sentences with these words.

| accommodation | apologise | equipment | facilities |
| punctual | reasonable | refreshments | register |

1 Are you going to <u>put your name down</u> for that new computer course? It starts next Monday.
2 The new school's <u>gym, concert hall and computer labs</u> are all in excellent condition.
3 I really feel I should <u>say sorry</u> for what I said to Amy – I didn't mean it.
4 Will there be any <u>food and drink</u> at the concert?
5 The prices in that shop are <u>quite cheap</u>, I think.
6 We will give you all the <u>things you need</u> for the activity.
7 I must say that Damian is always <u>on time</u> whenever we arrange to meet.
8 The <u>place you will stay</u> is in a small hotel by the sea.

Useful Language for Part 1!

words and phrases with opposite meanings, e.g.: borrow ≠ lend, after ≠ before, cheap ≠ expensive, etc
words and phrases with similar meanings, e.g.: want / like = be keen on, would rather, would prefer; out of order = not working, etc
things that are part of a particular group, e.g.: hotel = accommodation; pool, free Wi-Fi = facilities, etc

Reading 1

4 Read what the people said. Then circle the correct words so that the sentences say the same thing in a different way.

1 'I'm going to be in the school play!'
Marty's going to take **part** / place in the school play.

2 'I think everything has become more expensive in this shop recently'.
Prices in this shop have **increased** / decreased recently.

3 'We must book tickets for the theatre by Saturday!'
Please request / **reserve** your theatre tickets by Saturday.

4 'You have to pay £5 to get into the castle.'
The access / **admission** charge for the castle is £5.

5 'Does Paula know about the exam next month?'
I'm not sure if they have **informed** / interviewed Paula about the exam next month.

5 Look at the messages and notices. Choose the correct meaning, A or B.

A The train going to South Milton is leaving and passengers should hurry.
B The train to South Milton is going to arrive soon.

> THE NEXT TRAIN IS DUE ON PLATFORM 7. PASSENGERS FOR SOUTH MILTON SHOULD USE THE FRONT SECTION OF THE TRAIN.

1 ›

A Harry phoned to say that his guitar lesson is at three o'clock.
B Harry will have his guitar lesson before you go out together.

A You will be able to get your money back if you have not used the product.
B Money is given back even for products that you have used.

5 ›

> Please give Sally a ring.
>
> She wants to ask you about the dance practice this evening.

A According to school rules, students cannot use the library computer.
B The library computer is not working properly.

A Sally wants you to bring the ring she left at dance practice.
B Sally wants you to phone her about the dance practice.

4 ›

> Notice to all students. The library computer is currently out of order.

3 ›

> Unless you have used this product, you will be able to get a refund.

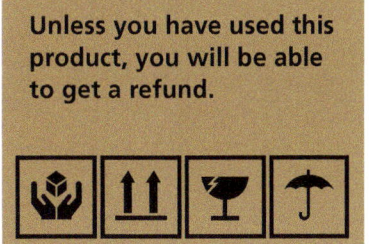

2 ›

> Harry won't call for you until three o'clock, after he's had his guitar lesson.

11

1 Reading

STEP 2 PRACTISE

1 Read the five texts. Choose the correct reason, a or b, why they have been written.

1

a) to give students a warning

b) to invite students to an event

3

a) to ask people for help

b) to give people some information

4

a) to give instructions

b) to sell something

2

a) to ask a friend to take a book back to the library

b) to ask a friend to give back a book that they'd borrowed

To start the coffee machine, plug it in and then press the red button.

In two minutes your drink will be ready!

5

a) to invite someone to have a drink

b) to explain how to operate something

Reading 1

2 ▸ Read the short texts 1-5. Write True (T) or False (F) for each sentence.

THIS TRAIN STATION CLOSED UNTIL FURTHER NOTICE.

ALL PASSENGERS PLEASE USE WHITECROSS STATION.

1

a) You and some other passengers missed the last train. T ☐ F ☐

b) You have to go somewhere else to catch your train. T ☐ F ☐

2

a) Lynne wants to go to the exhibition with Chloe. T ☐ F ☐

b) Lynne's Dad can take them both to the exhibition. T ☐ F ☐

From: Lynne
To: Chloe

Hi Chloe,

Are you going to that art exhibition with your Mum? If you are, can I have a lift? My Dad's away on business.

Thanks,
Lynne

Amanda – I'll be a bit late home from work today. Please switch on the cooker and prepare the vegetables. I'll bring the chicken with me.

Mum

3

a) Amanda should get the meal ready for her and her mother. T ☐ F ☐

b) Amanda should buy some chicken on her way home. T ☐ F ☐

4

a) Cars cannot get to the Town Hall at the moment. T ☐ F ☐

b) If you are walking, you can use the road as normal. T ☐ F ☐

No entry!
Castle Road closed to vehicles. Access to Town Hall by Queen Street only.

Yearly bus passes for students available now.

Application forms to be filled in by September 10th.

No late applications, please!

5

a) Students can use their old bus passes after September 10th. T ☐ F ☐

b) Students have to give their details in order to get a bus pass. T ☐ F ☐

13

1 Reading

STEP 3 PASS

EXAM TIP!

- Quickly read each notice and think about:
    the main message
    where you might see it
    why it has been written
- Use what you see as well as what you read to help you understand the meaning.

1 For each question, choose the correct answer.

Clare,

Tim rang. He's going to be late for the concert. He said you should go in anyway and he'll text you when he gets near the concert hall.

Mum

1
What should Clare do?

A text Tim before the concert starts

B not change her arrangements

C wait for him outside the concert hall

No access to pool Wednesday 27th October.

No lessons until further notice.

Open to public Thursday 28th October 10 a.m.

2

A No one can use these facilities on Wednesday.

B People having lessons can use the pool on Wednesday.

C The public can swim in the pool in the mornings only.

Reading 1

EXAM TIP!
- Read the three options A, B and C. Only one option will match exactly the meaning of what you have read.
- Check your answers before you move on to the next Part.

FOR SALE

Mobile phone + free cover

Used, no marks on screen

Special price this week only!

Phone Liz: 695004

3
The advert says that the mobile phone

A had a cover but it got lost.

B is currently a bit cheaper.

C has got a special type of screen.

THE HOLIDAY CARAVAN PARK

The Holiday Caravan Park

Bookings start from next Saturday, March 1st!

Minimum stay: 7 nights

No dogs or other pets please.

4

A Visitors to the caravan park usually stay for a week.

B It is now possible to book a holiday for March.

C Animals are not allowed in the caravan park.

5
What does Jake want to do?

A go and get Coco after his holiday

B leave Coco at Tom's until Friday

C ask Tom to bring Coco to his house

Hi Tom,
Thanks for looking after my rabbit Coco this week. We'll be back on Friday but late – around 11 p.m. Shall I come to your house and get him on Saturday? Will you be at home?
Jake

15

2 Reading

STEP 1 PREPARE

What's on this weekend?

WHAT YOU HAVE TO DO

In this part:
- you have to read about five people and eight different situations.
- you need to match each person to the correct short text.
- there are three extra texts that you do not need.

1 Look at the pictures. What's your favourite form of entertainment?

2 Complete the sentences with these words. You may need to make the word plural. There are two extra words you do not need.

| audience | channel | concert | comedy |
| documentary | headline | performance | recording |

1 Charlie Chaplin was one of the world's most famous actors. For many years, he acted in _____ , as did Laurel and Hardy.

2 Hollywood stars are used to having their names in the _____ – that's the price of fame!

3 Dana is new to the hip-hop scene but she gave a fantastic _____ last Saturday. I think she'll go far.

4 I don't always like _____ but the one on Sunday evening about the history of pop music was really good.

5 According to this article, the _____ at the Arts Theatre last night absolutely loved the show!

6 I heard that Lou and his friends are going to make a music video. Where are they going to do the _____ ?

Useful Language for Part 2!

matching similar information, e.g.: two weeks = a fortnight = fourteen days; realistic = true-to-life; small groups = up to five people in a group, able / ability / advanced = can do sth well, enjoy yourself = have fun, etc
verbs that express your wants and likes, e.g.: prefer, want to, would like to, be keen on, will need to, require, etc

3 Match the words 1-8 with their meanings a-h. Then complete the conversation about a concert with the words.

1 admission _____
2 advice _____
3 atmosphere _____
4 challenges _____
5 entrance _____
6 professional _____
7 review _____
8 variety _____

a an article that gives an opinion
b consisting of different types
c difficult situations
d the feeling in a place or at an event
e the cost of a ticket
f the way in to a building
g suggestions about what someone should do
h qualified or expert

Reading 2

Lucy: Phil, there are two bands playing at the weekend – can you give me any 1 _____ about which one is better?

Phil: Sure. Well, Magic Heads have had a lot of 2 _____ recently with one of the players injured in an accident. They're 3 _____ musicians, though, so they do their best.

Lucy: Hmm. How about The Crash? They usually play a 4 _____ of stuff, don't they? It's not all just the same sound all the time.

Phil: Yes, and there's always a really good 5 _____ at their concerts. I read a 6 _____ about the group and it said they were really good. And 7 _____ isn't too expensive, either!

Lucy: OK, I've decided – I'm going to see The Crash. Do you want to come too?

Phil: Yes, of course! I'll meet you outside the 8 _____ at 7 pm.

4 Jake and Polly want to watch a TV programme this evening. Read the texts and circle the three types of programmes they each like.

Jake likes thrillers, but he isn't allowed to watch them late at night. He doesn't mind watching comedies either. He finds quiz shows boring because they don't have enough action but he quite enjoys nature programmes.

Polly's favourite programmes are police dramas or detective films but she doesn't like horror films. She doesn't watch romantic films but she likes to test her knowledge in quiz shows.

5 Jake and Polly have chosen two possible programmes each to watch but only one is really suitable. Read the texts and tick ✓ the most suitable programme for each person.

Jake

☐ **1** *The House on 9th Street*
A clever film set in 1940s America, with lots of atmosphere and action. Not for those of you who get easily frightened because there are some scenes that will make you hide behind the sofa! On tonight at 10.00 p.m. after the national news.

☐ **2** *Crazy Pets*
You won't stop laughing during this show about animals who can't sit still and who won't do anything their owners tell them to! You won't get bored either because there's always something new happening. On this evening at 8.00 p.m., followed by the quiz show.

Polly

☐ **1** *101 Questions*
For all of you who want to learn something while you're relaxing, tonight's quiz is about countries of the world. Were you listening during your Geography lessons? Now's the time to find out! On tonight before Police Car at 8.30 p.m.

☐ **2** *The Search*
See if you know who the killer is in this exciting series set in 19th-century London. Some great acting from the main characters and amazing costumes from the period. A warning: some scenes may be a bit frightening for the younger audience. On tonight at 9.00 p.m.

2 Reading

STEP 2 PRACTISE

1 Read what three teenagers say about the type of books they would like to read. Note down the different types of book, choosing from the list below.

stories about real-life events   biographies   books with facts and information

fiction   books written by young people

science fiction   comic books

1 Mike would like to read about unusual things that teenagers like him have done, especially if they are written by the people themselves. He also enjoys stories about strange creatures that live on other planets!

Type of books Mike likes:

2 Susi enjoys novels about children or animals and she likes adventure novels because they make her dream of unusual things that might happen in her life! She would also like to read books that teach her something new about the world.

Type of books Susi likes:

3 Angelica wants to read books about famous people so she can learn more about their lives. But she also loves novels set in schools. Her hobby is collecting old picture stories, especially ones like the Beano.

Type of books Angelica likes:

2 Work in pairs. Discuss these questions.

What sort of books do you enjoy reading?

When you want to find out some information, do you use a book or the internet? Which is better?

Reading 2

3 Read the five advertisements for online booksellers and the type of books they sell.

a Underline the parts of the descriptions that match what the teenagers in Exercise 1 like.
b Choose the most suitable bookseller for each teenager.

Mike: _____   Susi: _____   Angelica: _____

A

Easy Reading

Our online store can offer you the top 100 novels each month! All types of fiction available, from detective stories to comics.

This week's top ten include *Shep the Sheepdog* and *The Mystery of the Missing Coin.* You won't be able to put this exciting story down!

Also don't forget our series of books about world geography and history – so many things you didn't know!

> **TIP!**
> - Some descriptions of the booksellers might partly match what the teenagers like.
> BUT you must choose the bookseller that matches <u>everything</u> they like.

B

Books for You!

Well-known authors, famous names, they're all here!

The biggest online bookstore and the best prices!

This month we are running our competition to find the best children's author – and you only have to be over 16! Science fiction, adventure, comic strip – you can write whatever you like.

Click on the link below for more details, and don't forget – **keep reading those books!**

C

Best Books

Shop here and choose from a huge variety of books. We particularly support new authors and young authors who have not been published before. Have a look at our new teen collection of real-life stories, plus our range of science fiction and schoolbooks.

Great news! Our online series of talks about fiction-writing starts next week!

D

Online book club

All your favourite authors at amazing prices: novels, short stories and comic books!

Also don't miss our Young Author of the Year series of prize-winning novels written by teens aged 11–14.

Want to find out more about someone well-known?

Click on a name and you're sure to find the book you want.

E

I  reading!

Books for teens and all ages.

As well as all types of fiction, we have wonderful encyclopedias and interesting biographies.

Look too at our special collection of rare comic books – all the old favourites.

This week's best-seller: Year 9 at Westburn High

2 Reading

STEP 3 PASS

EXAM TIP!
- Underline the key information.
- Read the descriptions of the people first.

For each question, choose the correct answer.

**The teenagers below all want to go to a summer school.
On the opposite page there are descriptions of eight music and dance summer schools. Decide which summer school would be the most suitable for the teenagers below. For questions 1–5, write the correct letter (A–H).**

1

Jen wants to improve her guitar-playing skills and her brother Toby is keen on learning different styles of piano-playing. Jen would also love some dancing lessons. They'd like a 14-day course.

_____

2

Vic already belongs to a street dance group but he wants to learn more. He thinks a week should be enough. If possible, he'd also like to start learning the piano.

_____

3

Cara is a teen champion in Latin American dances. She requires professional help to prepare her for international competitions. She is also interested in the history of dance. At the moment, she can spare two weeks, but no more.

_____

4

Vivi plays the violin but she'd love to have the experience of performing with others. Her parents are going abroad so she will need to spend a month at the school.

_____

5

Tomas has never played a musical instrument but he's got a good singing voice and he wants to learn how to control his breathing better. He'd like a two-day course.

_____

Reading 2

> **EXAM TIP!**
> - Remember that the option you choose must match exactly what each person likes, wants or is interested in.
> - Don't choose an option just because it contains the same word. You must look at the meaning of the whole text.

MUSIC AND DANCE SCHOOLS

A Star Quality
Many top performers have followed the Star Quality summer school. Classes include orchestra work leading towards a public performance in front of international artists. Other activities include modern dance classes. Street dance classes are very popular, attracting more than a thousand students every summer! The shortest course available is a ten-day course.

B One Tune
Students from this school say it's like a home from home for students who are away from their families. Teaching of singing and a variety of musical instruments is very strong, with many students going on to study professionally. Also very popular are the orchestral concerts that take place at the end of each four-week course.

C Quality Time
This school has an especially happy family atmosphere, with music teachers also helping to look after the students in the evenings. The school offers mainly dance classes but there are also advanced classes in the piano and the guitar. All courses are weekly

D Top Ten
This summer school offers a variety of classes for all levels. Two-week and one-month courses are available in music (all instruments) and dance for beginner, intermediate and advanced levels. Visiting professionals give training in classical and jazz piano techniques as well as voice control.

E Ace Academy
This is the place for all future stars! Dance, hip-hop and ballet are all taught, together with one-to-one instruction in singing techniques and classical music. Weekend courses available in July and August only. Group courses start every Monday.

F Sound System
One of the best summer schools in the country. It has classes in all instruments, including the piano. Students wishing to learn a new instrument are particularly welcome. Other courses include lessons about famous classical musicians of the past. Dance classes are led by professional and experienced dancers.

G Zed & Julie's
This school is run by a husband-and-wife team. Julie, a professional violinist, gives small classes to advanced students only. Zed is a judge on TV dance shows and teaches dance to students who want to compete at a high level. He also gives lessons in the background to different dances. Courses are normally 7 or 14 days.

H Performance X
Younger students really enjoy this school. It's got a very lively atmosphere and also produces some top-quality performers. Well-known street dancers give lessons to students who've already reached a good standard. Individual lessons are also provided in the violin and piano. Beginners are welcome in the music classes. Weekly classes only.

3 Reading

STEP 1 PREPARE

What's your favourite place?

WHAT YOU HAVE TO DO

In this part:
- you have to read a long text with five multiple-choice questions.
- you have to choose your answer from A, B, C or D.

1 Look at the places in the illustrations. Do you like visiting different places? Where do you like to go best?

2 Find the missing letters to match the words and the pictures.

1. ☐ b__y
2. ☐ b_ock of f_ats
3. ☐ cotta__e
4. ☐ harbo__r
5. ☐ o_ean
6. ☐ pal__ce
7. ☐ r__in
8. ☐ ea_th
9. ☐ stre__m
10. ☐ wat__rfall

a

b

c

d

e

f

g

h

i

j

3 Complete the sentences with words from Exercise 2.

1. Suddenly, in the middle of the forest, we discovered an amazing _____ that fell over a huge rock.
2. My grandparents live in a house, but we live in a _____.
3. We spent the afternoon looking at the fishing boats in the pretty, old _____.
4. Who was the last king to live in the _____ of Versailles?
5. There was a _____ at the bottom of the garden with fish in it.
6. Unfortunately, the castle we visited was a _____ – there were just a few stones to show where the walls used to be.

22

Reading 3

4 Replace the underlined parts of the sentences with these adjectives. You may need to add other words as well.

| challenging | curious | embarrassed | miserable | surprised | unable |

1. I missed the bus so I <u>couldn't</u> get to the department store before it closed.
2. The mountain walk was quite <u>difficult</u> at times, especially because I wasn't wearing proper walking boots.
3. It was raining hard and all the visitors to the town <u>weren't looking very happy</u>.
4. <u>I didn't expect</u> to see so many of my friends at the youth club last week.
5. It was awful when I slipped and fell into the river – I felt so <u>stupid</u>! It was lucky that the river wasn't very deep!
6. Liz <u>likes finding out information about</u> scientific facts – that's why she's got so many books in her room!

5 Read Jessica's story. Then write true (T) or false (F) for sentences 1-5.

Countryside experiences

I'm basically a city girl and I'm glad about that, but when I was growing up I was lucky because my parents took me on holiday every year, either to the seaside or the countryside. I particularly remember one holiday in a small village in a farming area of the country. My parents had rented a small cottage at one end of the village, next to a wood. Every day we used to go for a pleasant walk around the village, passing a farm with its particular farm smells! We explored the wood too, and I was delighted to discover a small waterfall right in the middle of it! Somehow the waterfall seemed to be alive to me and in the evening, before it got dark, I would go and say goodnight to the waterfall. Strange, wasn't it? But I know I never felt frightened in that wood.

1. Jessica feels unhappy that her childhood was spent more in the city. T ☐ F ☐
2. Jessica's parents owned a holiday cottage in a village in the country. T ☐ F ☐
3. Jessica enjoyed being in the countryside, despite the strange smells. T ☐ F ☐
4. Jessica wasn't afraid of going into the wood on her own. T ☐ F ☐
5. In this text, Jessica wants to give advice about living in the countryside. T ☐ F ☐

6 Work in pairs. Discuss these questions:

- Do you prefer living in the city or in the countryside?
- Where do you like to go on day trips?

Useful Language for Part 3!

adjectives that describe feelings or opinions, e.g.: annoyed, confident, glad, disappointed, brilliant, exciting, boring, etc

reporting verbs/expressions, e.g.: advise, warn, encourage, persuade, describe, request, realise, regret, suggest, etc

other phrases showing opinion and attitude, e.g.: enjoy, be keen on sth, be keen to do sth, be a pity that, be worth doing sth, not feel like doing sth, etc

3 Reading

STEP 2 PRACTISE

1 Read what three people say about places that are important to them. For questions 1–6, circle A or B.

A Adam, scientist

As a scientist and biologist, I've had the opportunity to work in many different regions of the world: the rainforests of South America, the mountains of Borneo and the African deserts. During that time I've learned to respect nature more. Previously, I'd thought that going to these places would be just like a walk in the park! In fact, I grew to understand that whoever goes there without proper preparation is not behaving responsibly, either towards themselves or the ones who care for them.

1 What is the writer's main purpose in writing the text?
 - **A** to warn readers that some trips require careful planning
 - **B** to encourage readers to travel to unusual places on holiday

2 How has the writer's attitude changed towards his work?
 - **A** He feels less confident about his abilities as a scientist.
 - **B** He is more realistic about the challenges that this type of travel involves.

B Bianca, sporty type

I suppose you could say that my second home is the local sports centre since I seem to spend most of my spare time there! I'm really keen on all kinds of sports so it would be difficult for me if we didn't live in the city near all the sporting facilities. You see, I want to become a professional sportsperson later on after studying Sports Science at university. Sport is my life!

3 What is Bianca's attitude towards living in the city?
 - **A** She feels negative about it because she is very busy all the time.
 - **B** She feels positive about it because it allows her to follow her interests.

4 What are Bianca's plans for the future?
 - **A** She would leave school now if she was offered professional training.
 - **B** She aims to carry on her education and then take up sport professionally.

C Mick, fishing fan

I grew up in a small village with just a post office and one small shop, so my friends and I had to find amusing things to do. We ended up walking across some fields and learning to fish in the river. When we went to secondary school, my friends started other sports but for me fishing had become a serious hobby. Now I take part in competitions as far away as Scotland so I no longer have to spend all my time in my small village!

5 What does Mick say about his attitude towards fishing in the beginning?
 - **A** He did it because there was nothing better to do at that time.
 - **B** He thought it might be something he could get really good at.

6 What might Mick say about fishing now?
 - **A** 'Fishing is something I enjoy when I have time and there's nothing better than sitting by the river near my village and enjoying the peace and quiet.'
 - **B** 'I never dreamt that fishing could lead to such an exciting life, travelling to new places and meeting new people. It's fantastic!'

2 Look back at questions 1–6 in Exercise 1 and answer these questions.
 - **a** Which question asks about why the writer is writing the text?
 - **b** Which question asks you to understand the general meaning of the text?
 - **c** To answer these questions, do you need to read a bit of the text or all the text each time?

Reading 3

3 Read the text about a school trip. For each question, choose the correct answer.

The Eden Project

14-year-old Gina Baptiste talks about discovering a rainforest

Last month I got the chance to visit the Eden Project in Cornwall, southwest England, on a school trip. This tourist attraction was opened to the public in 2001. Since the beginning it has been very popular and hundreds of thousands of people have visited it. It has to be one of the best trips I have been on. It's a fantastic place to visit if you are studying the natural world. I thought it would be just another kind of park but the biomes there were incredible! The biomes are those strange plastic shapes you can see in the photos. Some of them are up to 55 metres high! Inside them are over one million different types of plants from all over the world. My favourite was the Mediterranean Biome because the temperature is similar to that of Mediterranean countries, except it's right here in the UK. I also love olives and grapes. There were even birds flying around inside the biomes!

The whole of the Eden Project is completely environmentally friendly. They use rainwater throughout the project for watering the plants, wind energy for electricity and the sun for heating. We attended quite a few workshops about that which taught me a lot, but the one I enjoyed the most was about the rainforest. We learned how plants, people and animals all fit together in the rainforest. What I found the most interesting was how the people of the rainforests use the plants and trees for food, medicines and many other things. Generally, I thought the experience was fantastic and it has definitely made me understand the importance of the natural world and how humans should behave towards it. We depend on nature to provide us with food but now nature also depends on us to look after it.

> **TIP!**
> - Read the whole text quickly to get the general meaning.
> - Then answer each question.
> - The first 4 questions follow the order of the text.
> - The last question tests your understanding of the whole text.

1 What is Gina Baptiste doing in the first paragraph?

   A persuading other schools to go on a trip to the Eden Project
   B describing her experience on a recent trip to the Eden Project
   C giving advice on how young people can help the environment

2 What does Gina say about the Eden Project and the biomes?

   A It was nothing like she had expected.
   B The only things to see there were plants and trees.
   C It's best to visit during the summer.

3 What was Gina's attitude towards the Eden Project's workshops?

   A Her feelings changed as she took part in them.
   B She liked them less than other parts of the trip.
   C She found them a valuable learning experience.

4 What effect has the trip had on Gina?

   A It has made her want to find out a lot more about the rainforest.
   B It has made her feel more responsible for the environment.
   C It has made her want to become a vegetarian.

5 What might Gina write in her diary about the trip?

   A It's only worth going on the trip if you are studying the natural world or if you are a scientist.
   B The Eden Project is a brilliant place and has lot of plants, but there isn't enough to do there.
   C Going to the Eden Project was really educational. I now know much more about the environment around the world.

3 Reading

STEP 3 PASS

EXAM TIP!
- Read the text quickly then look at the questions.
- Read each paragraph carefully again and underline the part which answers the question.
- Mark your answer and check again before you move on to the next part.

For each question, choose the correct answer.

Discovering the past

14-year-old Jerome Benson writes about an interesting school trip.

A couple of months ago, I went on a school trip to South Wales. My history teacher led the trip since he said it was time we got out of the classroom and saw some living history! The trip took place over a weekend but I didn't mind that. It was a chance to see a bit of the countryside, as well as an opportunity – as my parents also said – to get me more interested in one of my lessons! Most of my friends didn't come since they didn't like the idea of 'wasting' a weekend looking at ancient ruins.

One place we visited was a very old town called Caerleon that dates back to the Roman period in the 1st–3rd century. In fact, walking around the small town with what remains of the old theatre, castle, baths and harbour on the River Usk, I found myself taken hundreds of years back into the past even though parts of the town are very different now, of course.

The following day, we visited a place called St Fagans National Museum of History, an open-air museum where historical buildings have been rebuilt stone by stone. Some of the buildings are used for traditional skills such as making horse shoes or creating items for the house out of iron, and you can walk around and watch the people at work. I know I couldn't work with iron because I'd be afraid of burning myself but some other kids in the group had a go. They were braver than me! Some other people used materials that they found in nature to make things. For example, there was one lady who used sheep's wool to create birthday cards which she sold online! The cards were so nice that I bought one for my mum who loves animals.

History lessons would definitely be more interesting if we could learn traditional skills or even just learn more about how to use things from the land. I think I'll suggest it to our teacher when we get back to school – he usually approves of new ideas!

Reading 3

> **EXAM TIP!**
> - If you read a word you don't understand, use the text around it to help you work out what it could mean.
> - If you're not sure about which option is correct, based on the text, cross out the ones that are really not possible.

1. What was Jerome's attitude towards the school trip to South Wales?

   A   He didn't understand his teacher's reasons for arranging the trip.
   B   He wasn't happy that only a few of his friends came on the trip.
   C   He felt it was a pity that it happened during the weekend.
   D   He thought it might benefit him with his schoolwork.

2. How did Jerome feel about visiting Caerleon?

   A   It was a place where it was easy to imagine life long ago.
   B   It was too small to be of any real historical importance.
   C   He would have liked to spend more time there.
   D   It had changed too much in modern times.

3. What did the writer find especially interesting about the National Museum of History?

   A   He loved the opportunity to make things out of iron.
   B   He enjoyed helping to build a traditional house out of stone.
   C   He was very keen on products that had been made by hand.
   D   It was small enough to see everything they wanted to in a day.

4. After the trip, Jerome plans to

   A   work harder at his history lessons.
   B   request a change to the way history is taught.
   C   ask his teacher's opinion of open-air museums.
   D   visit more historical places like Caerleon.

5. What might Jerome write in his diary?

   A   It was exciting to be involved in what people used to do in the past but it's easier to learn historical facts through books at school.
   B   Learning about the Romans is important because we've done it at school. The river trip was pleasant too, since we saw the town better that way.
   C   The places we visited were great but I was disappointed that we spent so much time in museums.
   D   The trip wasn't at all boring, despite my friends' fears. In fact, I suddenly seemed to understand what history was all about.

4 Reading

STEP 1 PREPARE

How do you stay healthy?

WHAT YOU HAVE TO DO

In this part:
- you have to read a long text with five multiple-choice questions.
- you have to choose your answer from A, B, C or D.

1 Look at the photos and answer the questions.
- What are the sports facilities like where you live?
- What's your favourite food or snack? Do you think it's healthy?
- Do you have any hobbies? What are they?

2 Complete the sentences with these words.

| athlete | campsite | champions | competes | cruise | fit | gymnastics |
| jogging | keen | membership | part | score | sightseeing | sunbathe |

1 William has got really _____ on _____ in the park recently – but I think he's only doing it so he can keep _____ for football!

2 The _____ was fantastic! We went all around the Mediterranean and there was lots of time for _____ when we stopped at the ports.

3 Abby _____ in table-tennis competitions, she's the top swimmer at her school and she's won a gold medal in _____ She's an amazing _____!

4 _____ of the club is open to teenagers aged 13–18. They must be willing to take _____ in all the sporting activities of the club.

5 The final _____ was 5–0. We were the _____ again!

6 Since you're staying at that _____ by the sea, why don't you go water skiing or surfing? All you do is _____ all day long!

3 Complete the statements with words from the box. There are two extra words you do not need.

| cooker | dessert | herbs | ingredients | recipe | refreshments | slice | vegetarian |

1 After the meeting, there will be some light _____ .

2 I'm afraid I can't eat this meat – I'm a _____ .

3 _____ are often added to food to give it flavour.

4 This is a very popular _____ when it's hot outside!

5 These are some of the _____ you need to make a pizza.

6 Here's the _____ for carrot cake that you wanted.

Reading 4

Useful Language for Part 4!

Words/phrases with similar meanings, e.g.: not be interested in/not be keen on sth = dislike sth; throw away = get rid of; funny = amusing; feel like doing sth = be in the mood to do sth; soon = without delay, can't afford/not cheap enough = (too) expensive, etc

Reference words, e.g.: this/that, however, they/it, in this way, also, their, his/her, for example, etc

4 Tick ☑ the sentence, a or b, that has a similar meaning to the first sentence.

1 ▸ She isn't very keen on eating fast food.
  a She definitely prefers healthy food.
  b It is quite usual for her to eat fast food.

2 ▸ They shared a keen interest in sport.
  a Sport didn't have any real importance for them.
  b Their love of sport was something they had in common.

3 ▸ I didn't know that he was famous – you didn't tell me!
  a You left out the fact that he was a well-known personality.
  b He thinks he's well-known, but he isn't really.

4 ▸ Josh wanted to have some professional swimming coaching but it was too expensive.
  a Josh couldn't afford to have a professional swimming coach.
  b Josh's swimming coach was able to give him lessons for free.

5 ▸ By the time we got to the school concert, there wasn't enough room for us to sit.
  a The school concert was in a room where everyone stood and watched.
  b We arrived late and all the seats were taken.

5 Read the text about an organisation called Teenage Foodies. Then read sentences A-C and match them to gaps 1-3 in the text. Underline the parts of the text that help you to find the answers.

A It isn't necessary to have a good knowledge of cooking in order to take part.
B In this way, teenagers can become more independent in their food choices.
C The aim is for teenagers to improve their performance in sports.

d

e

f

Teenage Foodies is an exciting new organisation that gets teens involved in making their own decisions about what to eat and how to keep fit. **1** _____

The organisation was started a couple of months ago by Jake Morris, who wants to share what he knows about foods that help you to become physically stronger.

2 _____

Now he wants to hear from teenagers who might be interested in his work and join him in some 'cook-ins': that is, cookery classes he runs where he gets the audience to join in!

3 _____ Jake would actually rather hear from kids who understand very little about food preparation, but who are keen to learn in a fun atmosphere.

29

4 Reading

STEP 2 PRACTISE

1 Read the text quickly and answer the questions.

Young chef competition

The competition

For the third year, this popular competition is back! Readers of our magazine are invited to send in a recipe of their own, together with a photo of the finished dish, which they should prepare and cook themselves. **1**____ If sending by email, please attach the photograph together with the recipe in a separate document.

Competition rules

You can choose what type of food you would like to cook: it can be a main course or a dessert. All ingredients must be fresh and easily available according to the season. After you have made your dish, you should taste it to make sure that the recipe works. The recipe should not use ingredients that are too expensive so watch your spending carefully. **2** ____

The final date for electronic entries is March 31st. You can send in your entries any time after March 10th. Postal entries must arrive at our offices by March 29th. Please allow at least three working days for your entry to get to us by post.

The winning recipe

We will publish the lucky winner's recipe, and prize, in the June issue of our magazine. **3** ____ This can be taken any time between June and September 30th of this year.

1. Where can you read about the cookery competition?
2. What do you need to do to take part in the competition?
3. What type of food should be used in the competition?
4. By what date should you send in an entry by email?
5. Where will the winner be able to see their winning entry?

2 Now match three of the sentences A-D below to gaps 1-3 in the text. There is one extra sentence you do not need.

A The total cost of the dish should come to a maximum of £10.
B He or she will also enjoy a free meal for two at Farmhouse Food restaurant.
C What is important is that the dish should taste nice, never mind the cost.
D Entries for the competition can be sent either by email or by post.

> **TIP!**
> - Identify the main topic of each paragraph.
> - Look for clues that will help you find the missing sentence.

Reading 4

3 Read the text about a squash player, Jacki. Then match 4 of the sentences A-F below to gaps 1-4 in the text. There are two extra sentences you do not need.

Jacki Pritchard – squash player

Jacki Pritchard, 16, is a squash player in the national youth team. Squash is a fast, indoor sport played in a court with four walls. For major, international competitions, the walls are made of glass so the spectators can watch the match!

Jacki first started playing squash when she was 11. **1** ____ Jacki's aunt was keen on the sport and she took her along with her one day to the courts she played on in the nearest town. 'I thought it was a fantastic game!' Jacki says. 'It's such fun because you can hit this little ball really hard and it just comes back at you.' Jacki soon started playing every weekend and after a few months, the squash coach at the club noticed her and offered to give her some lessons.

Since then, squash has become Jacki's main interest. **2** ____ 'Regarding my free time,' she says, 'I don't see it as giving up something nice for something difficult. My friends understand that, although they sometimes complain that they don't see enough of me.' **3** ____ She knows what she wants and that's to win matches for her team and her club.

As she lives in a small village on the coast, Jacki has to travel a lot and often has to get up really early to make a practice session at 9 o'clock in the morning. **4** ____ 'I couldn't do it without their support,' she explains. But she can't wait till next year when she can start driving lessons!

A Fortunately, her mum and dad don't mind taking her around in the car.
B Her answer is that they are with her all day at school so what's their problem?
C Her interest in the sport was largely due to the influence of a relative.
D Jacki's parents feel that she should spend less time playing squash.
E The members of Jacki's youth team are top players in the country.
F Training sessions have replaced Saturday evenings at the cinema.

4 Reading

STEP 3 PASS

EXAM TIP!
- Check carefully what comes before and after the gap.
- After you choose your answer, check why the other sentences would be wrong.

Five sentences have been removed from the text below. For each question, choose the correct answer. There are three extra sentences which you do not need to use.

Your World youth camps

Would you like to spend part of your summer holidays in a different and exciting way? Then why not try one of the *Your World* camps in the country of your choice? We usually take young people between the ages of nine and seventeen although in certain cases we may accept younger brothers and sisters.

1 ____ The reason for this is that part of each day is spent either doing a particular sport or learning a foreign language. The sports offered include football, horse-riding, tennis and table tennis. Sometimes a camp might teach a particular sport because of the place where it is. **2** ____ You therefore need to remember that when you make your choice.

You might want to choose a camp that is near to your home, or one that is in another country. **3** ____ In that way, parents won't need to worry. The languages offered at the camps are normally the local languages: Italian in Italy, French in France and so on. However, English is taught in all our camps and is the main language of communication.

Every day at the camps follows a similar pattern, so if you're a person who enjoys having a lot of freedom, this may not be the right place for you! However, the students who come to our camps normally enjoy having a busy timetable to follow. **4** ____

Meals are taken altogether in the dining tent where you can choose from a wide range of tasty dishes. **5** ____ This is so important for building relationships and a feeling of belonging. If there are certain foods that you don't like, you needn't worry. Our chefs prepare food that is suitable for children with special preferences so there will always be something for you on the menu.

We look forward to seeing you soon!

Reading 4

EXAM TIP!
- The missing sentence must fit grammatically. It must also match the meaning of the paragraph and the text as a whole.
- Re-read the text at the end to make sure it really makes sense.

A   It's a time when campers can relax and exchange their news.

B   We will arrange for someone to accompany you if you travel by air.

C   Teachers are available 24/7 to help with any problems.

D   Taking part in a particular sport is not based on your ability.

E   The programmes at our camps are divided in two ways.

F   It doesn't give the younger ones time to miss their families!

G   For example, we give diving instruction in the south of France.

H   *Your World* takes no responsibility for cancelled flights.

5 Reading

STEP 1 PREPARE

How do you like to travel?

WHAT YOU HAVE TO DO

In this part:
- you have to read a text with six missing words.
- you have to answer six multiple-choice questions and choose the correct word.

1 Work in pairs. Discuss these questions.
- Do you like travelling?
- What forms of transport have you been on?
- Have you ever travelled abroad? If you haven't, where would you like to go?

2 Complete the description of a journey with these words and phrases.

| airport | by air | cabin | check in | delays | duty-free | flight | immigration | luggage |
| on board | reservation | took off | | | | | | |

My parents had made our 1 _____ months before of course, so everything was ready for our trip. The problem about travelling 2 _____ is that quite often you have to get to the 3 _____ very early in the morning. My mum likes to be punctual so we all got up at 5.00 a.m. and arrived just over an hour later, in plenty of time to 4 _____. The 5 _____ was at 8.10 a.m. and we hoped there wouldn't be any 6 _____. While we were waiting we looked around the 7 _____ shops and bought a present for our friends in London.

The plane 8 _____ on time. 9 _____ we had a really good video to watch and the 10 _____ crew brought us a tasty breakfast. I was so hungry! When we arrived at London Heathrow Airport, we had to queue to get through passport control and 11 _____. However, we eventually got our 12 _____ and went outside. Our friends were there, waiting for us. We were very happy to see them!

3 Look at the pictures and complete the missing words in the dialogues.

1 A: Have a look at my new b _ _ _ _ _ _ _ _. It's really light, perfect for the walking holiday.
   B: Yes, it's fantastic! Oh, and don't forget to take a cap and s _ _ _ _ _ _ _ _ _ _ – they say it's going to be really hot next week!

2 A: My uncle had his w _ _ _ _ _ _ stolen on the underground train last week.
   B: Oh no! What did he do?
   A: He went straight to the police of course – and then went home by bus!

3 A: These s _ _ _ _ _ _ _ are really cool! Can I have them? You know my old ones are worn out, Mum, and they'll be great to travel in!
   B: OK, but don't leave them at the hotel like you did last year!

4 A: I think these s _ _ _ _ _ _ _ _ _ _ T-shirts will be useful – you can just put a s _ _ _ _ _ _ on over them if the evenings are a bit cool.
   B: I agree. I think I'll buy a few more in the sales.

Reading 5

4 Complete the sentences with the correct word from each pair.

1 **booking / accommodation**

   a I'm afraid I shall have to cancel our _____ for August 20th.

   b The _____ you requested is full. Here are some other suggestions.

2 **way / direction**

   a Which is the quickest _____ to the city centre, please?

   b What _____ do we want to go in? Towards the sea or towards the mountains?

3 **close / fasten**

   a _____ your seatbelts please, and switch off your mobile phones.

   b Your suitcase won't _____ because you've got too many clothes in it!

4 **very / absolutely**

   a The weather during our holiday was _____ awful so we decided to come home early.

   b During the afternoon, the sun was _____ hot and some people got burnt.

5 **crossroads / crossing**

   a The sea _____ was a bit unpleasant because it was so windy.

   b When you get to the _____, turn right and then first left.

6 **border / boarding**

   a _____ has now started for the flight to Paris. Please have your documents ready.

   b I think the _____ between France and Switzerland is just over there.

7 **confirmed / realised**

   a After we had set off, I _____ I had left the tickets on the kitchen table at home.

   b The pilot made an announcement and _____ our time of arrival at JFK airport.

8 **amount / total**

   a Despite the _____ of traffic on the motorway, we managed to get to the theatre on time.

   b Over 20 million tourists in _____ visited Venice last year.

> **TIP!**
> - Always read the whole sentence carefully before you choose your answer.

Useful Language for Part 5!

verbs/phrases/phrasal verbs, e.g.: make friends, take part in, spend time, have a party, depend on, carry on, etc
confusable verbs, e.g.: bring/take; ask/demand; develop/become; earn/gain; keep/remain; miss/lose, etc
confusable nouns, e.g.: total/amount; group/company; work/job; licence/permission; luck/chance, etc
confusable adjectives, e.g.: further/longer; similar/like; essential/needy; missing/absent; ordinary/usual, etc
confusable adverbs, e.g.: extremely/completely, definitely/absolutely; generally/fully; typically/commonly, late/lately, etc

5 Reading

STEP 2 PRACTISE

1 Read the sentences and choose the correct word, A, B or C, for each space.

1. What's the _____ transport like in your country?
   - A common
   - B personal
   - C public

2. We saw a helicopter _____ on the roof over there ten minutes ago. I wonder who was in it?
   - A landing
   - B driving
   - C boarding

3. I don't like any of this jewellery. Most of it looks _____ cheap.
   - A actually
   - B certainly
   - C terribly

4. I don't think these trousers _____ me any more – I've grown six centimetres since last year!
   - A match
   - B fit
   - C wear

5. What's the exchange _____ between the dollar and the pound right now?
   - A amount
   - B rate
   - C level

6. Is your father travelling to China on _____ or for personal reasons?
   - A business
   - B work
   - C job

7. They _____ off their shoes and socks and walked across the sand to the sea.
   - A put
   - B took
   - C got

8. All flights are _____ due to bad weather conditions.
   - A delayed
   - B announced
   - C missed

2 Check your answers to Exercise 1 and discuss why the other options were wrong.

> **TIP!**
> - Check the words before and after the gap.
> - The missing word might be part of a phrase or a group of words that go together.
> - Make sure the meaning of the word you choose is the correct one.

3 Read the text about fashion. For questions 1–6 circle A, B, C or D.

FASHION

Early 18th century fashion

Fashion is a strange thing. Each time it changes, we think the new styles have never 1 _____ before. We also think that every new fashion is much better than the previous one and that everyone who doesn't 2 _____ it is old-fashioned!

1. A shown
   B existed
   C been
   D designed

2. A keep
   B buy
   C wear
   D follow

In fact, fashions are repeated over the years. To prove this 3 _____, all you have to do is ask your parents what they wore when they were teenagers. There will surely be something that is 4 _____ to what you wear now. What's reasonably certain is that there won't be a lot of difference!

3. A point
   B topic
   C theme
   D question

4. A like
   B same
   C similar
   D familiar

One particular style that hasn't come back yet, however, is the fashion of the 18th century. No doubt everyone feels very glad about that. But I wonder what people's 5 _____ of our fashions will be in three hundred years' 6 _____? Who knows?

5. A thought
   B attitude
   C feeling
   D opinion

6. A age
   B period
   C time
   D future

5 Reading

STEP 3 PASS

EXAM TIP!
- Read the whole text quickly then look at the options.
- Choose your answer and think about why the other options are not correct.
- Check your answers before you move on to the next part.

PASS A

For each question, choose the correct answer.

Walking holidays

Walking holidays are popular these days. However, if you're going on one, then you need to be 1 _____ careful about the amount of things you take with you in your backpack! Choose your clothes according to the 2 _____ of weather expected in the area you are going to. A few cotton T-shirts and shorts should be enough in most warmer countries in the summer. Bottles of things like shampoo are heavy so perhaps suggest 3 _____ as a group rather than each person taking their own. Other things to 4 _____ are any necessary travel documents.

Don't set off on your journey without having a 5 _____ idea of where you are staying and how you aim to get there. You won't feel so anxious if you know that there is a room waiting for you at the 6 _____ of the journey. When you can relax comfortably after a long day, planning ahead never felt so good!

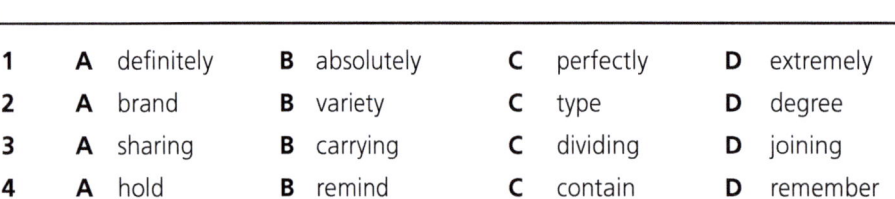

1	A	definitely	B	absolutely	C	perfectly	D	extremely
2	A	brand	B	variety	C	type	D	degree
3	A	sharing	B	carrying	C	dividing	D	joining
4	A	hold	B	remind	C	contain	D	remember
5	A	strong	B	clear	C	clean	D	perfect
6	A	finish	B	arrival	C	end	D	destination

Reading 5

> **EXAM TIP!**
> - You can try to complete the gaps before you look at the options.
> - Then look at the options and see if any of them match what you were thinking of.
> - Read the sentence with the gap to yourself with the option you think is correct. Does it sound right?

PASS B

For each question, choose the correct answer.

Lost luggage

My family and I had been looking forward to our holiday on the island of Menorca all winter and now we were on our way! From the plane as we **1** _____ the island, I could see sandy beaches and the clear blue sea. Everything looked **2** _____ perfect.

We therefore **3** _____ such a shock when they told us at the airport that our luggage was not on the plane. There had been a **4** _____ and it had gone somewhere else! I got cross, my father **5** _____ explanations but it was no good. We had to go to the hotel and wait for our luggage to appear – which it did, three days later! Meanwhile, we also had to buy some clothes but the weather was hot and we didn't need many. Of course, the first thing I bought was a swimming costume – and I fell into the sea, and the pool. But I was so glad to see my favourite pair of denim shorts again when I **6** _____ got my suitcase back!

1	A	arrived	B	approached	C	flew	D	returned
2	A	actually	B	clearly	C	very	D	absolutely
3	A	did	B	took	C	had	D	gave
4	A	reason	B	mix	C	fault	D	mistake
5	A	demanded	B	asked	C	called	D	said
6	A	lately	B	finally	C	lastly	D	slowly

6 Reading

STEP 1 PREPARE

How digital are you?

WHAT YOU HAVE TO DO

In this part:
- you have to complete 6 gaps in a text with one word.
- you do not have any extra words to choose from in this task.
- you use your knowledge of the language to find and write the missing word each time.

1 Discuss these questions.
- What's your favourite subject at school? Why?
- How do you use technology useful for your learning at school and at home?

2 Complete the sentences with these words or phrases.

| break up | curriculum | economics | handwriting | lab |
| nature studies | qualifications | register | | |

1 Are we doing experiments in the chemistry _____ this afternoon?

2 What _____ do you need to get into university?

3 They're talking about making some changes to the _____ next year.

4 _____ is an interesting subject and very useful if you're thinking of having a career in business.

5 If you want to _____ for the summer language course, please give your name to the school secretary by the end of the week.

6 It's difficult to read your _____ – please make it clearer.

7 We're going on a walk in the forest for our _____ lesson tomorrow.

8 What date do we _____ for the summer holidays?

3 Circle the correct words.

1 Don't forget to **switch off / switch on** the computer before you go to bed.

2 The internet **communication / connection** was rather slow last night.

3 By mistake, Maria **downloaded / deleted** some important work on her laptop and had to do it all again.

4 If you don't want to use the mouse so much, you can learn to use the **keyboard / screen** more.

5 The computer really is an amazing **equipment / invention**.

6 Matt wasn't answering his phone but I expect he'll **switch it on / call back** later, when he sees that I've rung.

7 I can't remember the **message / password** to get into this website.

8 Did you know that 'email' really means '**electronic / electrical** mail'?

40

Reading 6

4 Rewrite the second sentence so that it means the same as the first. Write ONE word in each gap.

1 At school, we are taught physics by Mr Thornton

   At school, Mr Thornton teaches _____ physics.

2 They put the desks in single rows for the examinations.

   The desks _____ put in single rows for the examinations.

3 Our class designed a new website last week!

   A new website was designed _____ our class last week!

4 Why don't you upload that new software?

   It would be a good idea _____ upload that new software.

5 We did all our written homework on the computer.

   All our written homework was _____ on the computer.

6 My job was to check that no computers were left on at the end of the lesson.

   My job was to check that the students _____ turned off all the computers at the end of the lesson.

TIP!
- Read the whole sentence or text.
- Think about the type of word that is missing in the sentence, eg preposition, adjective, verb, etc

5 Read the short text about Eton College. Circle the correct words to complete the text.

Eton College is one of **1 the / a** most famous schools in England. The school **2 is / was** started by King Henry VI in 1440. In the beginning, **3 there / they** were 70 students at the school. In those days, all the boys from Eton went to King's College, Cambridge **4 for / to** study. Sports such **5 like / as** football and cricket are really important at Eton and the students **6 be / are** also taught a wide variety of musical instruments. They perform concerts and plays every year.

Useful Language for Part 6!

Verbs/helping verbs, e.g.: know (how to do sth), did/have/had/are, would, be (keen to, etc), have (a lesson), have to do sth, etc
Passive, e.g.: was born, were invented, is connected, etc
Prepositions/prepositional phrases, e.g.: want to do sth, at school, on the internet, information about sth, be fond of / keen on, good at, etc
Relative pronouns, e.g.: who, which, where, when, etc
Pronouns, e.g.: it, them, their, me, etc

Comparatives, e.g.: more than, not much, the most, etc
Conjunctions, e.g. so, but, because, etc
Phrasal verbs, e.g.: switch on, call back, break up, turn off, sign up, take up, etc
Other phrases, e.g.: have no/not much time (to do sth), have an effect on sb, such as, be famous for, more than, apart from, one day, there was/were, why don't you …?, for a long time / for ages, every week, since/for, etc

6 Reading

STEP 2 PRACTISE

1 Read the sentences. Then choose the correct word from the pairs of words in the box and write it in the gap.

be / was
he / they
for / in
no / not
than / but
that / where

1 Everyone in the class was very interested _____ the lesson on digital photography.

2 The computer _____ Sara was trying to lift was too heavy.

3 Fortunately, my school is _____ very far from my home.

4 It's easier for me to write on a computer _____ with a pen or pencil.

5 The teacher was angry with the children because _____ were speaking loudly in the library.

6 Emily _____ given a new smartphone for her birthday.

2 Read the text message from Luke to Ben. Then write the missing words in Ben's reply. Look at Luke's message for clues!

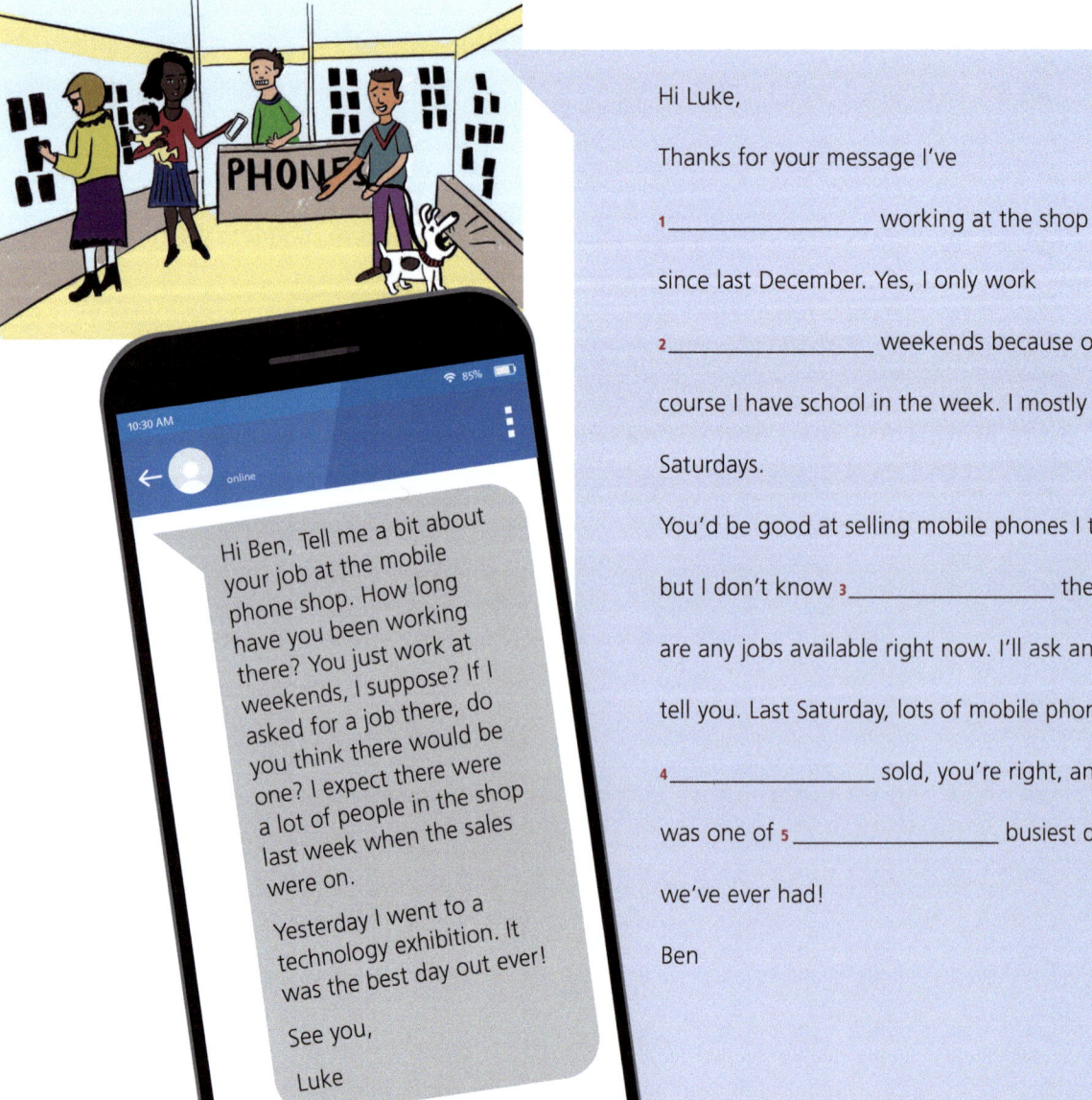

Hi Ben, Tell me a bit about your job at the mobile phone shop. How long have you been working there? You just work at weekends, I suppose? If I asked for a job there, do you think there would be one? I expect there were a lot of people in the shop last week when the sales were on.
Yesterday I went to a technology exhibition. It was the best day out ever!
See you,
Luke

Hi Luke,

Thanks for your message I've

1_____ working at the shop

since last December. Yes, I only work

2_____ weekends because of

course I have school in the week. I mostly do

Saturdays.

You'd be good at selling mobile phones I think

but I don't know 3_____ there

are any jobs available right now. I'll ask and

tell you. Last Saturday, lots of mobile phones

4_____ sold, you're right, and it

was one of 5_____ busiest days

we've ever had!

Ben

Reading 6

3 Read the three short texts and complete the gaps with ONE missing word. Use the tips to help you!

We asked three students to tell us why they enjoy learning. Here is what they said.

TIP!
- Look for phrasal verbs or adjectives followed by prepositions.
- Remember to think about helping verbs, eg was/were, did, have, etc.
- Read the text again to check your answers.

TEXT A

Nicole, 14

We often go on family holidays to Spain 1 _____ when we had to choose to learn Spanish or Italian at school, of course I chose Spanish! I love learning Spanish because I hang 2 _____ with some Spanish teenagers when we are on holiday and I feel really good when I can say something in their language! I also think it's important 3 _____ learn more about other countries as well as our own. That's why I'm reading some books now about Spain and 4 _____ history and culture.

TEXT B

Harris, 13

I enjoy learning about music because that's what I love most. At the moment, I'm having lessons in three instruments: the piano, the guitar and the drums. My poor parents don't get 5 _____ peace at home! I 6 _____ up the drums only recently and it's a great way to get rid of all that stress! My favourite instrument is the piano but I 7 _____ really like to play the keyboard in a band when I'm older. Already some friends of mine 8 _____ talking about forming a group so let's see what happens!

TEXT C

Becki, 12

One of my main hobbies is finding websites, I like 9 _____ the internet where I can learn more things. Of course, I have my favourite subjects – and other subjects that I am not so 10 _____ of so I focus on the subjects that I like. I've 11 _____ lots of books as well, especially about dinosaurs and whales. 12 _____ you ever visit science museums? I think they are fantastic. My parents took me to one last month and I didn't want to go home afterwards!

43

6 Reading

STEP 3 PASS

> **EXAM TIP!**
> - Read the whole text first quickly to get the main idea.
> - If there is a title, use it to help you to understand the context.,
> - Check your spelling: the word you write must be spelt correctly.
> - Read the whole text again to yourself and check your answers.

PASS A

1 For each question, write the correct word. Write ONE word for each gap.

Starting at a new school

By Mike Yates, 13

Thanks to all of you who are reading my blog! I hope you'll find it useful. Actually, I've been at my new school **1** _____ nearly a year now so I can look back and see what I did right.

Firstly, I decided **2** _____ join lots of societies and clubs. Sports are **3** _____ really my thing but I like table tennis. The first time I played, I met Tom, who has now become **4** _____ best friend! He and I really enjoy hitting the ball as hard as we can and winning – but we always have a laugh about it afterwards.

You could say I'm a bit geeky because I love finding things out on the internet – just weird facts about things. At the end of the second term, I **5** _____ asked by my teacher to go on my class quiz team – and we won the cup! But now it's nearly half term and I can't **6** _____ to go camping with the school. Things are looking good!

Reading 6

> **EXAM TIP!**
> - Remember you might have some question forms or suggestions in the text.
> - Check carefully what comes before and after the gap, and in the whole sentence/paragraph/text.
> - Always answer every question even if you are not 100% sure.

PASS B

Hi Ana,

I'm really pleased that Ms Williams put us together to work on our photography project. **1** _____ you done any research for it yet? I'm going to start doing something at the weekend – **2** _____ won't be any time before that!

Of course we really need to get out there and start taking some fab photos! In the town, apart **3** _____ the obvious castle and river, where else do you think we could go? It would be good to get some photos of some less well-known areas. **4** _____ about a visit to a local farm? I'd love to focus on a place where **5** _____ can show the importance of wildlife and a respect for the environment.

I've found some apps **6** _____ could be really helpful for our project. I'll give you the information as soon as possible.

Speak soon,

Liz

Reading

PERFECT!

What's in the Reading exam?

6 Reading Parts

How long does it last?

45 minutes

What do you have to learn before the exam?

- Grammar
- Vocabulary
- Useful phrases, words that commonly go together

In the exam:

- Don't panic!
- Read all the texts carefully – but not too slowly!
- <u>Always</u> write an answer even if you are not 100% sure.
- Don't forget the time. You <u>must</u> finish all 6 Parts.

1 Look back at Parts 1 – 6. In your own words explain what you have to do in each Part.

	I have practised this and can do it!
In **Reading and Writing Part 1** I have to …	☐ ☐
In **Reading and Writing Part 2** I have to …	☐ ☐
In **Reading and Writing Part 3** I have to …	☐ ☐
In **Reading and Writing Part 4** I have to …	☐ ☐
In **Reading and Writing Part 5** I have to …	☐ ☐
In **Reading and Writing Part 6** I have to …	☐ ☐

Reading

2 Read the important points below and add ONE more of your own for each Part.

Perfect Part 1 – *Pages 10-15*

- Read the notice or message. Why was it written?
- Think carefully about your answer and check it again.

- _____

Perfect Part 2 – *Pages 16-21*

- Be careful! The texts say similar things so check your answers carefully.
- You need to find the details that give you the correct answer.

- _____

Perfect Part 3 – *Pages 22-27*

- Understand how the writer is expressing feeling and opinion.
- Read each paragraph carefully and think about your answer. Is it the one that matches best what you have read?

- _____

Perfect Part 4 – *Pages 28-33*

- As you quickly read the text, think about how each paragraph moves the text forward.
- Carefully check the previous sentence and the sentence after the gap in order to find the correct missing sentence.

- _____

Perfect Part 5 – *Pages 34-39*

- Read the text quickly and think about the topic and the different events that are described.
- Use your knowledge of grammar and vocabulary or phrases to choose the correct answer.

- _____

Perfect Part 6 – *Pages 40-45*

- Read the text quickly and think about the type of word that is missing each time.
- Read each sentence carefully before and again after you write the missing word.

- _____

Now you'll be perfect!!

1 Writing

STEP 1 PREPARE

What can we do to help the environment?

WHAT YOU HAVE TO DO

In this part:
- you have to read an email which has four notes attached to it.
- you then have to write an email in reply, including all the points in the notes.
- the email might be informal (to a friend) or semi-formal (to a teacher, etc).

1 How is climate change affecting the weather? How can we help to protect the environment? Discuss your answers.

2 Complete the sentences with these words. You will need to make changes to some of the words.

branch	cliff	climate	dolphin	environment
freeze	nature	pollution	rainforest	range
recycling	rubbish	scenery	sunshine	

1 It's very important to protect the _____ of South America and the animals that live there.

2 We can help to reduce the _____ of the _____ by _____ our _____.

3 We were amazed to see brightly-coloured birds sitting on the _____ of the trees.

4 The _____ of Central Australia is very dry.

5 The place in the UK that has the most _____ is Jersey, with an annual average of five hours a day.

6 When the lake _____ in the winter, we go ice-skating!

7 What's the _____ of mountains in Northern Italy called?

8 Some city children don't have much contact with _____ and don't even know where their food comes from.

9 The _____ as we approached the coast, with huge _____ and thousands of seabirds, was fantastic.

10 I would love to go swimming with _____!

3 Complete the sentences about the weather with the correct words. The beginning of each word is given.

1 Tomorrow there will be __sh_____, especially in the morning, so take an umbrella with you.

2 The __f_____ was so thick that the traffic was moving very slowly.

48

Writing 1

3 There was a huge __s_____ last night. Did you hear the __th_____ and see the __l_____ ?

4 What's the __te_____ going to be like on Saturday? Will it be warm enough for a picnic?

5 The lake was __fr_____ yesterday and then it snowed overnight. Today, the __f_____ is for another __sn_____ !

6 In the recent __g_____ , two trees at the bottom of the garden were blown down.

> **Useful Language for Part 1!**
>
> **Agreeing,** e.g.: that's a good idea, I think you're right,
> **Apologising,** e.g.: I'm really sorry but …, I'm afraid that …, It's a pity but I …, Unfortunately, it's impossible because …, etc
> **Describing / telling,** e.g.: The weather was really good, We had a fantastic time, The food there was excellent, etc
> **Disagreeing,** e.g.: Sorry but I don't really agree, I'm not sure about that, I don't think that's possible, etc
> **Explaining,** e.g.: You see, I had to …, Actually, it was …, We couldn't … because …, That's why …, etc
> **Giving advice / recommending,** e.g.: You should …, It would be a good idea to …, I think you ought to …, etc
> **Giving an opinion,** e.g.: It would be lovely to (do, etc) …, I think (that) …, , I agree (that) …, In my opinion, …, I'd rather (do/not do, etc) …, etc
> **Inviting,** e.g.: Would you like to …?, It would be lovely if you could …, Can you …?, Are you free next XX?, etc
> **Offering,** e.g.: Shall I …?, Would you like me to …?, I can/could …if you like?, etc
> **Suggesting,** e.g.: Why don't you/we (go, etc) …?, Let's (have, etc) …, How about (visiting, etc) …?, etc
>
> You can find more functional phrases on pages 140.

4 Read some sentences from email messages. What is each sentence doing? Choose functions from the Language Box.

		Functions
1	You see, I couldn't come to the party because there was too much snow.	explaining
2	Can you come with us on a trip to the mountains next week?	
3	I'm sorry I forgot to take any photos of the flowers for you.	
4	How about asking your teacher if you can plant a few trees?	
5	We found a cave in the cliffs which was quite big.	
6	I'm really upset about the change of plans and I hope you don't mind.	

5 In your notebooks, write three short email messages using the situations 1-3 below. Include two sentences from Exercise 4 in each message.

1 You went to some lovely flower gardens but you forgot to take any photos of them for your mother. Write an email to your mother, apologising for not taking the photos and suggesting going with her another day.

2 You went to the beach last Saturday and explored the cliffs. Write an email to your friend Max, describing what you saw and inviting him to come with you next time.

3 Your friend Alice has written to you asking how her school can help the environment. Write an email to Alice, telling her what you have done at your school and suggesting what she could do at her school.

49

1 Writing

STEP 2 PRACTISE

1 Choose the correct word to complete the sentences.

1. Why don't you _____ around later this evening?
   A will come   B come   C coming

2. Many _____ for your invitation.
   A thank you   B thanking   C thanks

3. I'm not sure _____ I agree with you.
   A for   B if   C about

4. Yes, let's _____ shopping at the weekend!
   A go   B to go   C going

5. I'll meet you at the bus stop if you _____ .
   A are like   B will like   C like

6. I think that's _____ great idea!
   A one   B a   C the

7. How _____ going to the cinema tomorrow evening?
   A about   B much   C far

8. It was really good to _____ from you again.
   A get   B hear   C receive

9. What exactly _____ your plans for the trip?
   A will   B be   C are

10. _____ you got any spare tickets for the concert?
    A Do   B Shall   C Have

TIP!
- Remember to start and end your email with appropriate phrases, e.g. Hi Emma, Dear Mrs Trent, etc; Bye for now, See you soon, Best wishes, etc.

TIP!
- Try to learn some set phrases you can use in your email.
- Check your verb forms: -ing or infinitive?

2 Match the two halves of the sentences.

1. I'd recommend
2. Text me when
3. I'm looking forward
4. It will be difficult
5. I think we should
6. It's a pity that

a. to seeing you again.
b. meet inside in case it rains.
c. bringing a light jacket with you.
d. you missed the concert.
e. you arrive at the station.
f. to get there by 8 o'clock.

Writing 1

3 Read the sample exam task below. Look at the notes 1-4 and think about what you need to say in your reply.

Read the email and the notes from your friend Martin. Write a reply in about 100 words.

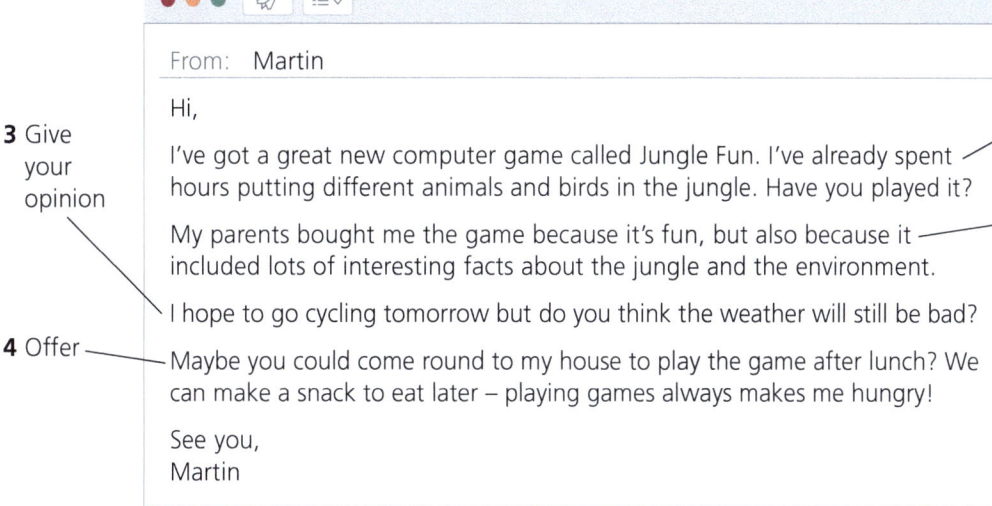

From: Martin

Hi,

I've got a great new computer game called Jungle Fun. I've already spent hours putting different animals and birds in the jungle. Have you played it?

My parents bought me the game because it's fun, but also because it included lots of interesting facts about the jungle and the environment.

I hope to go cycling tomorrow but do you think the weather will still be bad?

Maybe you could come round to my house to play the game after lunch? We can make a snack to eat later – playing games always makes me hungry!

See you,
Martin

1 Tell Martin
2 Cool!
3 Give your opinion
4 Offer

4 Choose the best way of expanding the notes 1-4, a or b. Explain your choices.

Note 1
- a No, I didn't buy it last year. I like watching sports programmes best.
- b No, I haven't played it but I've heard a lot about it.

Note 2
- a It sounds like a really good game.
- b OK but I hope it's not like having a geography lesson!

Note 3
- a If it's sunny tomorrow, I'm going to play football with Alec and George.
- b I've looked at the weather forecast and I don't think it's going to be sunny tomorrow!

Note 4
- a Why don't we go out to a pizza place to eat? That's more fun!
- b I could make some sandwiches if you like and bring them along.

> **TIP!**
> - In your reply, try not to repeat exactly the same words as those used in the email.
> - Remember you will have to add some extra information (explanation, description, etc) to bring the word count up to 100 words.

5 Write your email, using information from Exercise 4 to help you.

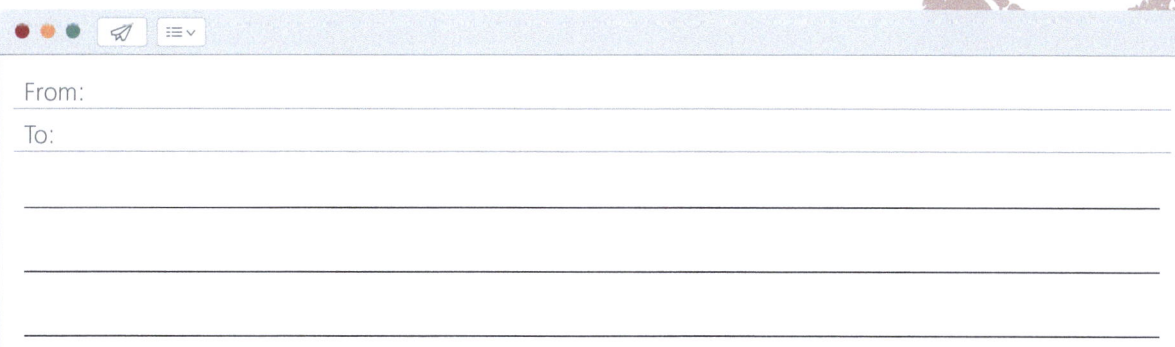

1 Writing

STEP 3 PASS

EXAM TIP!
- Read the email carefully. Understand who the person is writing to and why.
- Read the notes and think about what you must say in your reply.
- Organise your email into paragraphs.
- Check your email after you have written it for any silly mistakes!

PASS A

You must answer this question.
Write your answer in about 100 words.

1 Read this email from your English friend Kate and the notes you have made.
Then write your email to Kate using all the notes.

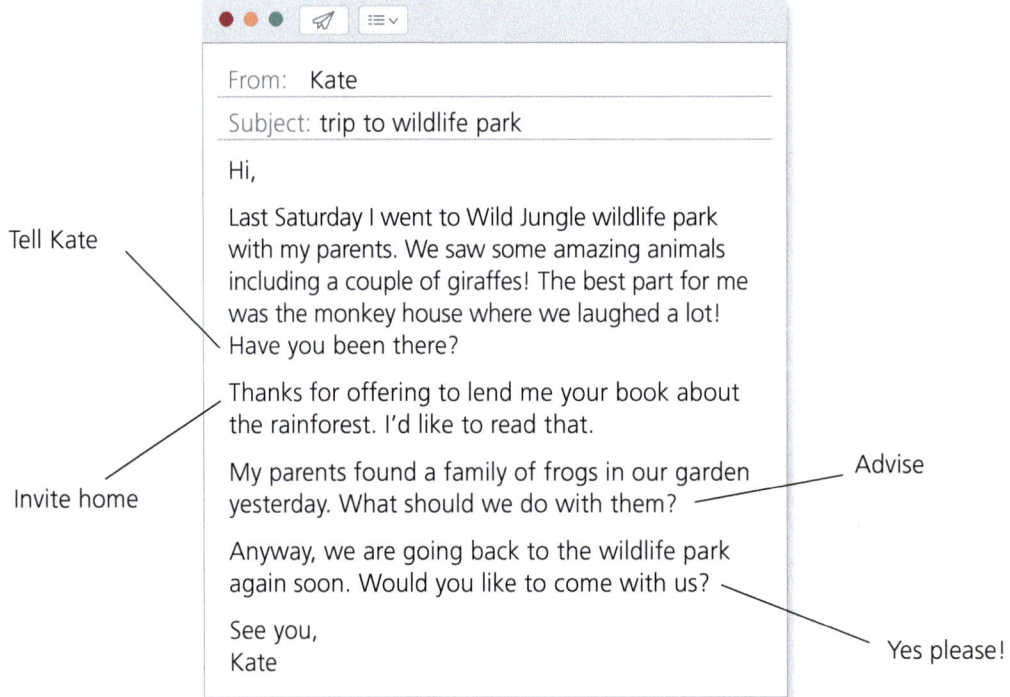

From: Kate
Subject: trip to wildlife park

Hi,

Last Saturday I went to Wild Jungle wildlife park with my parents. We saw some amazing animals including a couple of giraffes! The best part for me was the monkey house where we laughed a lot! Have you been there? — *Tell Kate*

Thanks for offering to lend me your book about the rainforest. I'd like to read that.

My parents found a family of frogs in our garden yesterday. What should we do with them? — *Advise*

Anyway, we are going back to the wildlife park again soon. Would you like to come with us? — *Yes please!*

See you,
Kate

Invite home

Writing 1

> **EXAM TIP!**
> - Make sure you include all 4 points in your reply. Expand your points with reasons and explanations or added information.
> - Check the word count of your reply. It should be about 100 words.
> - Try to show what you know: use a variety of words, expressions and grammatical forms.
> - Remember to use correct opening and closing phrases.

PASS B

You must answer this question.
Write your answer in about 100 words.

2 Read this email from your English teacher and the notes you have made.
Then write your email to Mr Mayfield using all the notes.

From: Mr Mayfield
Subject: school farm

Hi,

I wanted to tell you that the plan for a school farm has been approved! This will be a great opportunity to talk in English together while working on the farm. — *Fantastic news!*

We are having our first meeting for students after school on Friday. I hope you can come along then. — *Sorry, but ...*

I will be looking for a group of student volunteers to help out on the farm. How do you think we could find some helpers? — *Suggest*

Have you got any experience of working on a farm at all? — *Tell Mr Mayfield*

Best wishes,
Mr Mayfield

2 Writing

STEP 1 PREPARE

How fit and healthy are you?

WHAT YOU HAVE TO DO

In this part:
- you have to write EITHER a story OR an article.
- you should write about 100 words.
- for the story, you are given the first sentence.
- for the article, you have to read an advertisement which includes some information and some questions.

1 Look at the pictures at the top of this page.
- What are the people doing?
- What types of exercise do you enjoy?
- Which don't you like? Give your reasons.

2 Complete the sentences with these words. There are two extra words that you do not need.

1. I hope Carol recovers quickly from the _____ on her hand. I think I'll send her a get-well card.

2. There must have been an _____ on the motorway earlier – I saw an _____ going that way as I was driving home.

3. You feel very hot. I think you must have a _____ .

4. The _____ services came a few minutes ago and carried the injured footballer off the field.

5. I put my foot in a hole when I was out jogging and broke a _____ in my _____ . It was really _____ but it feels better with the _____ on.

6. The doctor gave me a _____ for some medicine. I hope it's not horrible!

```
accident     ambulance
ankle        appointment
bandage      bone        emergency
ill          operation   painful
prescription temperature
```

3 Read the advice page in a magazine. Complete the missing words.

I'm always so happy when winter is over and we can enjoy the warmer weather again! Gone are all the

₁ c _ _ _ _ _ _ and ₂ c _ _ _ _ _ and heavy coats and jackets. Of course, I'm sure you know the best way to fight a cold? You need to eat ₃ h _ _ _ _ _ _ _ _ and try to ₄ r _ _ _ _ . Vitamin C is really important so you should drink lots of fresh orange juice. Sometimes it can take a week or so to ₅ r _ _ _ _ _ _ _ from a bad cold or ₆ f _ _ and feel ₇ w _ _ _ again, so you just have to be patient. It's often wise not to do too much ₈ e _ _ _ _ _ _ _ _ _ while you are ₉ i _ _ . Take it easy until you are completely ₁₀ b _ _ _ _ _ .

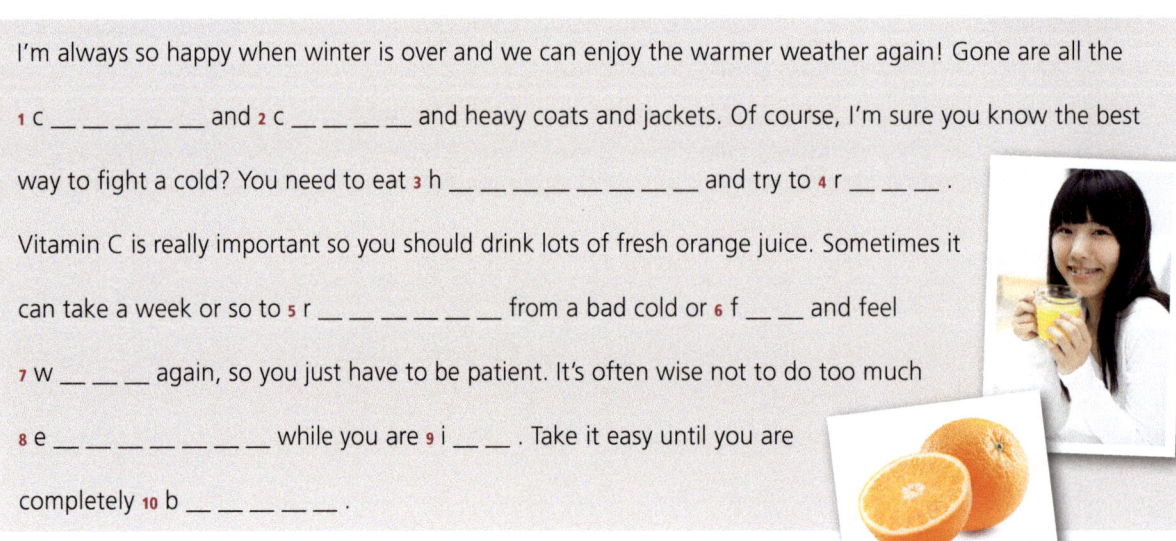

Writing 2

> **Useful Language for Part 2!**
>
> **Story:** narrative tenses, e.g.: past simple, past perfect, past continuous; linking/time expressions, e.g.: at first, then, after that, finally, suddenly, soon (after), before/after, one day/evening, last Saturday, when/while, a few minutes later, etc.
>
> **Article:** giving an opinion, e.g.: I think, I believe, In my opinion, etc; giving reasons, e.g.: because, since, that's why, etc; giving examples, e.g.: for example, for instance, such as, like, etc.
>
> You can find more useful phrases for writing stories and articles on p.141

4 Put these sentences from a story in the correct order. The first sentence from the story (1) is done for you.

	Dad had fallen asleep and he had driven the boat onto a rock at the edge of the lake!
	Fortunately, there wasn't much damage to the boat, but we all felt very silly when we took the boat back to the owner at the end of the afternoon!
1	Last weekend, the weather was lovely and we thought it was a great day for a boat ride on the lake!
	So we all got in the car and Dad took us to the lake.
	After about a quarter of an hour, there was a loud bang!
	When we got there, we hired a small boat and we all sat back and relaxed.

> **TIP!**
> - Check your past tenses.
> - Use suitable time phrases to connect your story.

5 Now write a story about a time when things didn't go quite right for you. Look at the story in Exercise 4 to help you. Read your story to a friend!

6 Read about Helen's favourite form of exercise. Add in the correct punctuation and capitalisation.

my main hobbies are listening to music hanging out with my friends and gymnastics I started doing gymnastics when I was very young and I've always loved it I go to gymnastics club after school every friday and I also go to another club on saturday mornings my coach, helen francis, took part in the olympics some years ago and she's brilliant in june I'm going to be in a schools gymnastics competition and I'm already getting nervous

2 Writing

STEP 2 PRACTISE

Writing a story

1 Complete the story about a mountain adventure with the correct form of the verbs in brackets. Use the past simple, past continuous or past perfect.

I was walking in the mountains with my father when suddenly we **1**_____ (see) a helicopter in the distance. A few minutes later, it **2**_____ (land) in a field at the bottom of the mountain. We **3**_____ (go) over to have a look and we **4**_____ (discover) that a woman climber **5**_____ (fall) and injured herself. She **6**_____ (lift) into the helicopter and it **7**_____ (take off) for the hospital. We **8**_____ (carry on) walking but then it **9**_____ (start) to get foggy and we **10**_____ (can) not see anything. While we **11**_____ (wonder) what to do, the fog **12**_____ (clear) and we **13**_____ (realise) that we **14**_____ (walk) in a circle! Finally, we **15**_____ (be) back where we **16**_____ (start)!

2 Now read the sample exam task for a story, and the answer written by a student. Complete the story with words from the box. There are four extra words you do not need.

| a | and | are | at | but | however | hurt | injured | to | too | was | were |

Your English teacher has asked you to write a story. Your story must begin with this sentence:

Stella was surprised when the doctor told her to do more exercise.

Write your **story**. Write about 100 words.

Stella was surprised when the doctor told her to do more exercise.

She thought she was quite fit **1**_____ perhaps she sat at her computer **2**_____ much in the evenings. Anyway, she decided to go to street dance classes twice **3**_____ week with some friends and at first they all enjoyed it. **4**_____, one evening they **5**_____ learning something a bit difficult and Stella fell onto her knees. Her knees **6**_____ a lot and she couldn't carry on. So she had a break for a few weeks and decided **7**_____ find out about other types of exercise. Maybe street dance **8**_____ the wrong choice for her!

56

Writing 2

Writing an article

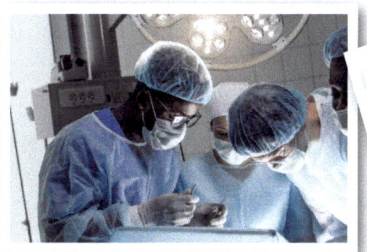

3 Read what three young people say about training as a doctor. Do you agree?

1 I'd like to become a doctor because I want to help people to live healthier lives. In my opinion, a doctor is one of the most important jobs in our society.

2 I admire doctors, but I don't think I could become one. Obviously, their job is extremely important – without them, people would not recover from their illnesses! But you have to be the right kind of person with certain qualities, like being calm and patient, and I don't think I am.

3 If you train as a doctor, you have to work long hours for many years. You also have to deal with a lot of stress. However, I think what keeps you going is the knowledge that somehow, you are making people's lives a bit better.

4 Look at the questions below and the article written by a student. Complete the article with one missing word in each gap, using Exercise 3 to help you.

TIP!
- Articles are organised into paragraphs.
- They are not a personal story although personal opinions can be given.

What is a doctor's life like? Would you like to be a doctor? Why/why not?

In my 1 _____ , a doctor's life is a difficult one

2 _____ it involves a lot of 3 _____

and long working hours. Doctors who work in hospitals have to

4 _____ with emergencies so they must have the right 5 _____ as a person. For

example, they have to keep 6 _____ and be patient when people are upset and need their help.

I admire doctors but I don't want to become one. Firstly, I'm not good at sciences and secondly, I want to

become a teacher. That will be my way of helping my students to get more 7 _____ and making

it possible for them to have 8 _____ lives.

57

2 Writing

STEP 3 PASS

> **EXAM TIP!**
> - Read the information carefully. Underline what you have to write about in your article.
> - Try to use your own words in your article as far as possible.

PASS A

Write an answer to one of the questions in this part. Write your answer in about 100 words.

Question 1

You see this notice in your school English-language magazine.

> **Favourite sports**
>
> Write an article telling us about the sports you like.
> What sports do you play?
>
> Which is your favourite sport? Why?
>
> *The best articles answering these questions will be published next month.*

Write your **article**. Write about **100 words**.

> **EXAM TIP!**
> - Read the introductory sentence carefully. Decide who your story will be about – is it 'I/we' or 'he/she'?
> - Make your story interesting for the reader. Show the language that you know.

Question 2

Your English teacher has asked you to write a story. Your story must begin with this sentence:

> *I was out jogging with my friend Poppy when she suddenly screamed and fell down.*

Write your **story**. Write about **100 words**.

Writing 2

> **EXAM TIP!**
> - Watch your timing. Don't spend too much time on one answer and then not have enough time for the second.
> - Check your answers for grammar, punctuation and spelling.
> - Choose the writing task that you think you know most about and that you like best.

PASS B

Write an answer to one of the questions in this part. Write your answer in about 100 words.

Question 1

You see this notice in your school English-language magazine.

> **Keeping fit**
>
> Write an article telling us about how you keep fit. Why is it important to you?
>
> What things should we not do if we want to be fit and healthy?
>
> The best articles answering these questions will be published next month.

Write your **article**. Write about **100 words**.

Question 2

Your English teacher has asked you to write a story. Your story must begin with this sentence:

I was going to buy a new toothbrush from the chemist's when something funny happened.

Write your **story**. Write about **100 words**.

59

Writing

PERFECT!

What's in the Writing exam?

2 Writing Parts

How long does it last?

45 minutes

What do you have to learn before the exam?

- Grammar
- Vocabulary
- Phrases for writing your email, and your article or story

In the exam:

- Don't panic!
- Remember all the important words and phrases you have learnt.
- Divide your time equally between the two parts.
- For the email and the article, make sure you answer ALL the points or questions.
- For the story, make sure you continue the story correctly from the first sentence that is given. Use correct tenses.

1 Look back at Parts 1 – 2. In your own words explain what you have to do in each Part.

I have practised this and can do it!

In **Writing Part 1** I have to …

☐
☐

In **Writing Part 2** I have to …

☐
☐

Writing

2 Read the important points below and add ONE more of your own for each Part.

Perfect Part 1 – *Pages 48-53*

- Read the email and the notes carefully.
- Use your own words in your email as far as possible.
- Show what you know – grammar, vocabulary, phrases!
- _____

Perfect Part 2 – *Pages 56*

Article

- Read the information given carefully and underline the points you need to answer.
- Plan your article, using paragraphs.
- Give your ideas and include, where possible, examples from your personal experience.
- _____

Perfect Part 2 – *Pages 57*

Story

- Think before you write! Make a quick plan of your story. Think about how you will make it interesting to the reader.
- Check your use of tenses:
- past simple for each event
- past continuous for description of what was happening at that time
- past perfect for events that had already happened
- Show what you know! Use some interesting vocabulary and phrases.
- _____

Now you'll be perfect!!

Title:

The beginning

The middle

The end

1 Listening

STEP 1 PREPARE

How do you help out at home?

WHAT YOU HAVE TO DO

In this part:
- you have to listen to seven short audio recordings.
- there is one question per text and three images.
- you will listen and choose the image that best answers the question.

1 Look at the chores the people in the pictures are doing.
- What are the chores called?
- How often do you do this kind of housework?
- What other things do you do to help out at home?

2 Put the words in the box in the correct category.

| the chores | the housework | the dishes | the ironing |
| a cup of tea | your bed | the laundry | the shopping | lunch |

make	do

3 Complete the sentences with the correct form of the verb in brackets.

1. Pete's mum had to work late, so he wanted to surprise her by _____ dinner. (prepare)

2. Fred's room was a mess, so his mother _____ that he tidied it up before going to bed. (suggest)

3. Lily is a bit strange – she loves _____ the bathroom! (clean)

4. Paul avoids _____ in the kitchen by saying he's got so much homework to do. (help)

5. Phil remembered _____ his grandmother a birthday card. (send)

6. Vicky isn't an early bird – she hates _____ in the morning. (get up)

Useful Language for Part 1!

In this part of the test you are tested on getting the key information from short dialogues or monologues. You will hear a wide range of functions and vocabulary, e.g.:
Instructions, e.g.: do, go, take,
Part of a presentation, e.g.: first, then, after that, I'd like to tell you about:
Announcements, e.g.: the train is arriving at platform 3, the shop is closing in 10 minutes
Making reservations, e.g.: I'd like to book…, Can I make a reservation, please?
Groups of words, e.g.: chores, food, clothes

Listening 1

 4 Holly is helping out by doing the shopping. She has made a shopping list. Look at the pictures, listen and write what is on her list.

 5 Listen again. Which items on Holly's list in Exercise 4 does she not need? Put a cross ☒ next to those items on the list above.

Holly: So, I'll go off to the supermarket now, Mum. Is there anything else you want?

Mum: Um, wait a minute, Holly. Let me just check the list: butter, flour, eggs – oh look, Holly, there's a new bag of flour at the back of the cupboard, I'd forgotten about that!

Holly: OK, so I'll cross that out, then.

Mum: ... and there's half a bar of chocolate here too, that should be enough for the cake.

Holly: OK, great.

Mum: Now the vegetables. Just have a look by the front door, Holly – did your father bring those potatoes from the farm?

Holly: Yes, they are there, so I won't need to buy any. Is that it, then?

Mum: I think so. You'll need to buy the rest.

Holly: Fine. See you later!

6 Read about Holly's day being helpful in the house. Circle the correct words.

Last Saturday, Holly's mum wasn't feeling very well so Holly decided to be helpful and do the **1 housework / homework** for her. First, she put some water in a **2 jug / kettle** to boil so she could make her mum a cup of tea. Then, Holly put all the dirty plates from breakfast in the **3 dishwasher / washing machine** and turned it on. After that, she tidied the **4 pillows / cushions** on the sofa where she and her brother had had a fight in the morning. Then she decided to try and iron some **5 sheets / carpets** as they had guests coming to stay for the night. Finally, Holly felt really tired, so she took a pizza out of the **6 oven / freezer** to cook for lunch and then went to ring her friend Susie.

1 Listening

STEP 2 PRACTISE

 1 **Listen to four short recordings and answer the questions.**
1. What are the girl and boy discussing?
2. What is Lizzie's problem?
3. What does Eddie's mum want him to do?
4. What is the girl's father trying to do?

 2 **Listen again and tick ✓ the correct answer, a or b.**

1. What will the boy put in his room?
   - a a wardrobe
   - b an armchair

2. What did Lizzie take to school with her?
   - a her tracksuit and hockey boots
   - b her swimming costume

3. What type of sandwiches is Eddie going to have today?
   - a cheese and lettuce
   - b chicken and tomato

4. What will the man buy?
   - a a clock
   - b a chest of drawers

Listening 1

3 Listen to five short recordings. Match two of the pictures (a–j) to each recording (1–5).

a ☐ b ☐ c ☐ d ☐ e ☐

f ☐ g ☐ h ☐ i ☐ j ☐

4 Listen again. For questions 1–3, write T (true) or F (false) for each sentence. For questions 4–5, circle the correct answer, A, B or C.

1.
   A At the sale next weekend they are going to sell jewellery, among other things. T ☐ F ☐
   B They are going to sell sports equipment at the sale next weekend. T ☐ F ☐
   C You will also be able to buy home-made cakes at the sale next weekend. T ☐ F ☐

2.
   A The flat didn't have a TV. T ☐ F ☐
   B The flat had a view of the sea but no balcony. T ☐ F ☐
   C The flat had a DVD player which they could use. T ☐ F ☐

3.
   A The competition this year is to design a new school uniform. T ☐ F ☐
   B Students will still have to wear a tie as part of the school uniform. T ☐ F ☐
   C Students will be able to choose to wear trousers if they wish. T ☐ F ☐

4. What is Hannah going to eat?
   A steak T ☐ F ☐
   B fish T ☐ F ☐
   C pasta T ☐ F ☐

5. Which sport did Mike do best in?
   A long jump T ☐ F ☐
   B running T ☐ F ☐
   C high jump T ☐ F ☐

65

1 Listening

STEP 3 PASS

EXAM TIP!
- Read the questions carefully so you know what information you will be listening for.
- Look at the images, identify the differences between them and try to predict the language that you might hear in the listening.

There are seven questions in this part.

For each question, choose the correct answer A, B or C.

Example: Where are the candles?

A   B   C

1 What sport is the boy going to learn?

A   B   C

2 What does the girl need to buy?

A   B   C

3 What is the last programme on this evening?

A   B   C

Listening 1

> **EXAM TIP!**
> - Be careful! There are distractors in this part, and you might hear all three images mentioned, but only one will be the correct answer.
> - When you hear the conversation again, look back at the pictures to check that the first answer you chose is right.

4 Where did the girl leave her mobile phone?

　A　　　　　　　B　　　　　　　C

5 Who is the girl phoning?

　A　　　　　　　B　　　　　　　C

6 What does the boy need most?

　A　　　　　　　B　　　　　　　C

7 What did the girl do before she watched television?

　A　　　　　　　B　　　　　　　C

2 Listening

STEP 1 PREPARE

How are you feeling?

WHAT YOU HAVE TO DO

In this part:
- you will listen to six short dialogues.
- you will be provided with a sentence to set the context and a question.
- you need to choose the option which best answers the question.

1 Look at the people in the photos and discuss these questions with your partner.
- Where are they?
- What do you think just happened or is about to happen?
- How do you think they might be feeling?
- When have you felt the same way?

angry	happy	sad	relaxed	bored
frightened	excited	embarrassed	lonely	
miserable	jealous	curious	patient	amazing
serious	disappointed	lucky	nervous	
confident	brave			

2 Choose adjectives from the box in Exercise 1 and decide how the people below might be feeling and why.

1 'I don't think I'm going to pass my maths test.'

2 'We're going on holiday on Friday.'

3 'I can't speak Spanish at all, and I'm going to Spain tomorrow.'

4 'This is the longest film I've seen in ages, and nothing is happening.'

5 'I hope my boss doesn't find out!'

3 Work in pairs. Discuss these questions.

1 When was the last time you were embarrassed by something?

2 Do you consider yourself a lucky person? Why?

3 In what kind of places do you like to relax?

4 What is the most amazing adventure you've had?

5 What kind of things make you angry?

Listening 2

4 Using the adjectives from Exercise 1, how do you think these two friends feel?

5 Now listen to their conversation. How do the friends feel about the movie?

1 disappointed
2 frustrated
3 excited

6 Listen to the following dialogues. Write A if the speakers agree or D if they disagree.

1 > **A** I think this football team will win the championship.
   B I'm not too sure about that.
2 > **A** John is a great actor!
   B No doubt about it!
3 > **A** If we go to the beach, we'll definitely have fun!
   B You're absolutely right.
4 > **A** The Indiana Jones films are absolutely amazing!
   B I'm not too sure about that.
5 > **A** Maths is the most difficult subject at school.
   B That's for sure!
6 > **A** This was the best party ever!
   B I was just going to say that!
7 > **A** The Indiana Jones films are absolutely amazing!
   B I don't know if I agree with that.
8 > **A** I didn't like the food in the school today, how about you?
   B I thought it was really tasty!
9 > **A** I thought that was one of his best books.
   B Absolutely!
10 > **A** Have you heard their new album? It doesn't sound very inspired.
   B I beg to differ.

> **Useful Language for Part 2!**
>
> **adjectives that describe feelings or opinions,** e.g.: frightened, excited, nervous, miserable, etc
> **phrases showing agreement and disagreement,** e.g.: right, I agree with you, I think so too, are you sure? really? I don't agree, etc
> **phrases describing feelings,** e.g.: I'm feeling pretty nervous about…, I'm (not) looking forward to…, I'm so excited about….

69

2 Listening

STEP 2 PRACTISE

1 Listen and read the following dialogue. What do the speakers say about the following?

	Mariana	Freya
The location of the flat		
The decoration of the flat		
The change in the girl's lifestyle		

Mariano: How is your new flat?

Freya: It's great! We moved in last week and so far, it's been quite nice. My room is bigger than the one in the old flat and I really like the decoration. My parents chose a really nice colour for the walls. I guess the only thing is that it's much further from the school than the old flat, so now I have to get up an hour earlier.

Mariano: Wow, is it that much further? I would prefer to have a smaller room, but to be able to sleep longer!

Freya: Well, I really like my room now, so I don't mind waking up earlier. You have to come one day!

2 Now listen again and answer the question.

You will hear a girl telling her friend about her new flat. How does she feel about it?

A Pleased with the location.
B Happy with the size of her room.
C Upset about having to sleep longer.

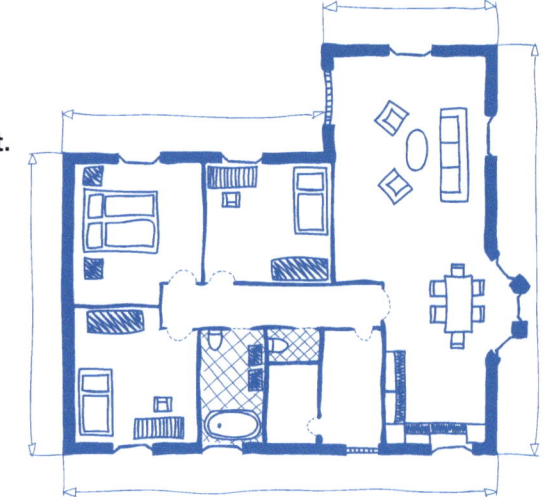

Listening 2

3 Listen and read the following dialogue. What do the speakers say about:

	David	Ellie
Learning Italian cooking		
The dishes		
What Ellie liked about the course		

David: Did you enjoy the cooking course last weekend?

Ellie: It was pretty good. We cooked a variety of Italian dishes, which is great because I didn't really know a lot about Italian cuisine.

David: That's great! Which recipe did you like best?

Ellie: We did a little bit of everything. The variety of salads and pasta dishes were really good and the sauces we made were very tasty but I what I really liked was making pasta by hand. I had never tried it and it was a lot of fun.

David: You must cook for me next time we meet!

4 Now listen again, and answer the question.

You will hear a girl telling her friend about a cooking course she went on. What did she like best about it?

A   The variety of pasta dishes
B   To learn about Italian cooking
C   Making hand-made pasta

2 Listening

STEP 3 PASS

> **EXAM TIP!**
> - Read the questions before you listen. Decide what you think you should listen out for.
> - On the first listening, focus on the main idea, and choose the answer. Then check the answer the second time you listen.

PASS A

1. You will hear two friends talking about a movie they have recently seen. They agree that

   A   the plot of the movie was boring.
   B   the ending was easy to guess.
   C   the actors were both very good.

2. You will hear a girl talking about a recent holiday with her family. Why did they decide to travel abroad?

   A   because of the facilities in the hotel
   B   because the hotel wasn't far from the beach
   C   because of the weather

3. You will hear two friends talking about the food served at a school party. They both agree that

   A   the food was very good.
   B   there wasn't enough food for everyone.
   C   they want to eat somewhere else.

4. You will hear a girl talking to her friend about learning Spanish. The boy advises the girl to

   A   look for a language exchange programme.
   B   buy a grammar book.
   C   do grammar exercises online.

5. You will hear two friends talking about a concert. They agree that

   A   the effects were good, and the fans knew the lyrics of the songs.
   B   the show was excellent.
   C   the singer was very good.

6. You will hear two friends talking about getting a new computer. The girl thinks that the boy should

   A   talk to the computer teacher.
   B   buy a new computer because the one he has is old.
   C   compare prices on the internet.

Listening 2

> **EXAM TIP!**
> - Remember that the adjectives used in the listening might be different to the ones used in the recording.
> - It's important to understand if the speakers agree or disagree.

PASS B

1. You will hear two friends talking about homework at school. They agree that

    A the teachers always give them too much homework.
    B the teachers give them too much homework some weeks.
    C the teachers sometimes don't give them enough homework.

2. You will hear a girl talking about a concert she went to on Saturday. How did she think was the worst thing about the concert?

    A that the stadium was so full
    B that the singer didn't sing in tune
    C that the tickets were so expensive

3. You will hear two friends talking about a football match. They both agree that

    A the other team's defense was weak.
    B it was an exciting match.
    C the score was very good.

4. You will hear two friends talking about their teachers. The boy thinks that

    A Ms Peters is interested in her students.
    B Ms Richards' lessons are easy.
    C Mr Lacey's lessons are serious.

5. You will hear two friends talking about a new app. The girl advises the boy to

    A play the game less often.
    B get rid of the app.
    C limit the number of levels he plays per day.

6. You will hear a boy talking about a punishment his parents gave him. The girl thinks

    A that his parents are being unfair.
    B that the punishment is quite reasonable.
    C that he is lucky because he will have more time for his school work.

3 Listening

STEP 1 PREPARE

How great is this town?

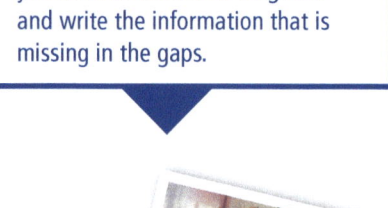

WHAT YOU HAVE TO DO

In this part:
- you have to listen to a long text and write the information that is missing in the gaps.

1 Look at the pictures and discuss the questions with your partner.
- What are the places called?
- What other places can you find in a town or city?
- Which or these places do and don't you like using?

2 Complete the sentences using the words in the box.

| bridge | square | corner | tunnel | turning | shopping centre |
| signpost | bus stop | fountain | roundabout | underground |

1 The Grand Hotel is the one with the _____ outside – it's really nice to sit by it on a very hot day! It's in the main _____ opposite the Opera House.

2 To get to the old _____ over the river, you have to go through the town, around the _____ and take the third exit. It's two minutes along that road.

3 There are usually some taxis right outside the _____ if you don't want to catch the bus. That's very convenient for people who've bought lots of things!

4 I'll meet you on the _____ of West Street and Sheep Street. There's a _____ near there for the town centre.

5 To get to Golden Beach, you need to drive five miles along this road. At the _____ that says 'West Bay', turn right and then take the second _____ for Golden Beach.

6 The _____ under the river is five miles long. If you don't use that, the journey will take you a lot longer.

7 The only disadvantage of travelling by _____ is that you can't see anything of the city.

Listening 3

3 Complete the crossword by looking at the clues.

Clues

Across ➡

1. A place where children like to play.
2. A place where you can stay if you don't live in this city.
3. A place where you go if you have a problem with your teeth.
4. A place where you can go to exercise.
5. A place where you can buy fresh food.
6. A place where you can go to admire works of art.

Down ⬇

1. A place where you go if you want to fly to another city.
2. A place where you can go if you want to borrow books.
3. A place where you can go if your hair is too long.
4. A place where you can go to watch a play.
5. A place where you can go to look at old things.
6. A place you can take money out of your account.

Useful Language for Part 3!

Linking words and phrases, e.g.: although, however, as well as, instead of etc.
Prepositions of place, e.g.: in, on, next to, opposite
Adverbs of frequency, e.g.: sometimes, never, occasionally
Phrases for talking about likes and dislikes, e.g.: I love, something I like to do is….
Giving and following directions, e.g.: Turn left, go straight on at…, take the first exit on the roundabout

4 Talk to your partner about a town they know well.

What do you like about the town you live in?

Lots of things. But the thing I love the most is definitely the park.

Why? What's so great about it?

It's really close to where I live, and there's always something exciting going on. What about you?

3 Listening

STEP 2 PRACTISE

1 Circle the correct words to complete these short dialogues.

1 **A:** You remembered to get the **bill / receipt** for the jeans, didn't you? You won't be able to take them back without it.

   B: Yes, I always make sure I've got it before I leave the shop.

2 **A:** I can't believe it! I won a competition recently and they gave me a **cheque / credit card** for £100 to spend at the All Stars shopping centre!

   B: Cool! If I come with you, will you buy me something as well?

3 **A:** Everything in this sports shop is too **expensive / reasonable**.

   B: Never mind. Let's go to Top Trainers, there's a sale on there.

4 **A:** My parents are always complaining about the cost of things these days.

   B: Mine too. But I know some really good online sites where you can get things at reduced **prices / cash**.

2 Listen to different people speaking and answer the questions.
1 What time did the concert start last year?
2 When does the dentist work on Wednesday?
3 What was the original price of a pair of shorts?
4 When did the girl want to start diving lessons?
5 Where is he taking his little sister?
6 What station should they not get off at?
7 How many seats are there on the coach?
8 Where are they going to meet?

3 Listen again and complete the notes.

1 This year's concert starts at: _____

2 Book dentist's appointment for: _____

3 Sale price of shorts: £_____

4 Diving lessons begin in: _____

5 Plan for this evening: go to_____

6 Station to get off at: _____

7 Number of students going on the trip: _____

8 In the square, you can use: a _____ to get money out.

4 Say and spell. Work with a partner.

A: Ask B to spell a word. **B:** Spell the word, then write it down.
Choose places, days or months.

How do you spell 'Thursday'?

T-h-u-r-s-d-a-y

OK. Now write it down!

76

5 ▶ Read the notes about a design competition. Before you listen, look at spaces 1–6 and think about what type of information is missing. Choose from these words and phrases. There are two extra items and you will need to use one item twice.

> amount of money   month   name (of person or thing)
> number   place   time   type of building

Design competition

Subject of competition: a new

1 _____ for the town

Entries must be in by the end of:

2 _____

The planned location for the new design is: opposite

Green 3 _____

The competition judges will be:

Chris Evans, Professor of Architecture

Emma Brown, editor of *Design* 4 _____ magazine

Designs for the competition should be: up to 5 _____ centimetres high

Prizes:

Second prize: design materials

First prize: one-month course at a design 6 _____

6 ▶ Now listen and check your answers. Don't try to fill in the spaces yet.

7 ▶ Listen again and fill in the missing information in Exercise 6.

3 Listening

STEP 3 PASS

EXAM TIP!
- Before you listen, look at the notes and gaps. Try to guess what kind of information goes in each one.
- Underline key words that show where you need to start listening more carefully.

PASS A

You will hear a teacher telling their class about a school trip to a museum. For each question, fill in the missing information in the numbered space.

School trip

Time the coach leaves from school: **(1)** _____

Choice of morning activities: Egyptian exhibition or **(2)** _____ exhibition

Maximum size of group for Egyptian exhibition: **(3)** _____ students

Lunch arrangements: either at a **(4)** _____ or bring food from home

What to bring with you: a **(5)** _____ and swimming costume if needed

Meeting place to go home: the **(6)** _____ outside the theatre

Listening 3

> **EXAM TIP!**
> - Check the spelling of your answers, especially if the answer was spelt out in the listening, as those must be correct.
> - Watch out for words that would possibly fit in the gap, but are not the right answer.

PASS B

You will hear a school principal telling a group of students about after-school music classes. For each question, fill in the missing information in the numbered space.

After-school music

Instruments you can study: Guitar (1) _____ and bass

To register: You have to bring a letter to (2) _____

The classes are on: Mondays and (3) _____

Cost: (4) £ _____ per class

Christmas concert: You can play a known Christmas song or an (5) _____

More information: Speak to (6) _____ or you can visit www.musicschool.net

4 Listening

STEP 1 PREPARE

What do you want to do later?

WHAT YOU HAVE TO DO

In this part:
- you have to listen to a longer text.
- you have to listen for specific information, opinions, attitudes and opinions.

1 Look at the photos and talk to your partner.
- Which of these jobs would you like to do? Why?
- Which of these jobs wouldn't you like to do? Why?
- What do you want to do later?

2 Match the photos of jobs to the words in the table by putting the right number in the first column.

Number	Job	1	2	3
7	chef	make a sauce	cook the vegetables	put the food on the plate
	hairdresser			
	politician			
	musician			
	police officer			
	farmer			
	pilot			
	reporter			
	receptionist			
	photographer			

3 Think of three things that each person has to do and write them in the table. Compare your ideas with other people in the class.

4 In pairs, take turns to ask questions and guess other jobs you can think of. Student A can only say "Yes" or "No"!

Do you have to talk to other people?

Do you sit down at work?

Do you have to make things?

Listening 4

5 Read the sentences and circle the correct word.

1 He **wins / earns** a lot as a company director but he also gives a lot of money to charity.

2 Fortunately, Tim gets on well with all his **colleges / colleagues** at work.

3 Have you filled in the **application / qualification** form for that job yet?

4 Before you sign the **contract / contact**, make sure you read it very carefully.

5 Mum works **full-time / part-time** as a school secretary – three days a week.

6 There were about a hundred **professionals / candidates** for the job they advertised last week.

7 Jenny hopes to have a **career / work** in television one day.

8 **A:** How many **employers / employees** does that company have?

   B: Over a thousand, I think.

6 Listen and match what you hear with these jobs. There are two extra jobs you do not need.

| architect | businessman | computer programmer | lawyer | lecturer | mechanic |
| novelist | publisher | reporter | soldier | taxi driver | travel agent |

1 _____

2 _____

3 _____

4 _____

5 _____

6 _____

7 _____

8 _____

9 _____

10 _____

Useful Language for Part 4!

making comparisons, e.g.: harder than, the most difficult thing is, X isn't as easy as Y, etc
verbs that you can use to talk about jobs and employment, e.g.: earn, employ, apply for, etc
talking about the past, e.g.: when I was young, I used to etc

4 Listening

STEP 2 PRACTISE

1 Listen and read. Then choose the correct answer, a or b to answer the questions.

Interviewer: Mel Barnes is a sixteen-year-old musician who plays the guitar and writes her own songs. Mel, tell us how you became interested in music.

Mel: Well, this was not something I had always wanted to do. When I was younger, in primary school, I spent most of my time outdoors, running and cycling everywhere! I was very active and I always had to be doing something. I thought piano lessons and things like that were a bit boring, to tell you the truth. Then, when I was twelve, I went to a music festival with some friends and I really loved it – suddenly I had to be part of the music scene!

Interviewer: So how did your life change after that?

Mel: Well, my parents weren't quite sure if I was serious about my interest in music, but they bought me a second-hand guitar, so I watched some videos on YouTube and gradually learned some simple songs. Then I started to write my own music and my own words. Of course this didn't all happen overnight and I had to keep up with my schoolwork at the same time. But a couple of years ago, I finally had some proper lessons and started taking guitar exams. That's when my parents realised that I meant what I said – I wanted to become a musician!

Interviewer: Tell us where you get the ideas for your songs from.

Mel: I've always read a lot and I think that helps with ideas and being creative. Mostly, however, I write about normal things that worry teenagers. Sometimes young people like me can find a lot of help through songs and music generally, so I hope that some of my songs do that.

1 What did Mel enjoy doing when she was younger?

   a sports

   b music

2 What made her interested in music?

   a her parents' influence

   b watching a public performance

3 How did Mel first learn how to play the guitar?

   a she had lessons

   b she taught herself

4 What convinced Mel's parents that she was serious about her plans?

   a the fact that she didn't fail any school exams

   b the fact that she had some proper instruction in her instrument

5 Where does Mel get most of the ideas for her songs from?

   a teenagers' problems

   b the books she reads

Listening 4

2 You are going to hear a girl called Alexia talking about her cake business. Read questions 1–4.

1 > Alexia's interest in food started because

   A   she enjoyed eating unusual things.

   B   she was bored at home all day.

   C   her mother encouraged it.

2 > What job did Alexia choose to do for her work experience?

   A   a chef

   B   a waitress

   C   a shop assistant

3 > While Alexia was doing her work experience,

   A   she came in at the same time every day.

   B   she always worked with the same team of people.

   C   she was helped by another member of staff.

4 > How did Alexia feel after her work experience ended?

   A   very disappointed

   B   quite positive about the future

   C   annoyed with herself

3 Now listen to Alexia and choose the correct answers in Exercise 2.

3 > Listen again and answer the questions.

   1   Why did Alexia prefer making cakes to cooking meals when she was young?

   2   What reason does Alexia give for choosing her particular type of work experience?

   3   What does Alexia say about the breakfast customers at the café?

   4   Where does Alexia normally sell the things she makes?

4 Listening

STEP 3 PASS

EXAM TIP!
- Read all the questions carefully before you listen.
- The questions usually use different words from those on the record, so expect to hear synonyms!
- In this part, questions about feelings are very common.

PASS

You will hear a boy called Jon Trenton talking about his experiences as a child actor. For each question, choose the correct answer A, B or C.

1 During the school holidays, Jon is allowed to act for
   A 12 hours a week.
   B 25 hours a week.
   C 14 hours a week.

2 Jon first got work in films through
   A his parents.
   B a teacher at his school.
   C a relative of his friend.

3 During his different acting jobs, Jon had most fun
   A in the detective series.
   B in the film with the dogs.
   C in the film in Scotland.

Listening 4

> **EXAM TIP!**
> - You will probably hear all the ideas in A, B and C, but they may not answer the question. Try and work out, not just which one is right, but which two are definitely wrong.
> - If you're not sure about an answer, try not to worry, and listen out carefully for this answer the next time you hear the recording.

4 What does Jon say about the making of a film?

   A The actual filming time is quite short.

   B The actors have to wait and often get bored.

   C The director's job is quite difficult.

5 When Jon was talking to the make-up artist, he was amazed by

   A how long she'd had that particular job.

   B how long he had to sit there.

   C how long putting make-up on sometimes took.

6 What does Jon say about some of his friends?

   A They realised that he'd become a different person.

   B They eventually became curious about what he did.

   C They never spoke to him again.

Listening

PERFECT!

What's in the Listening exam?

4 Listening Parts **25** Questions

How long does it last?

about **30** minutes

What do you have to learn before the exam?

- Listen for specific information
- Listen for gist
- Locate and record specific information

In the exam:

- Arrive at the exam venue with plenty of time.
- Make sure you read the instructions very carefully.
- Answer as many questions as you can the first time you listen.
- Check your answers. The second time you listen, answer the questions you couldn't answer on the first listening.
- Transfer your answers from the question paper to the answer sheet at the end of the test. You will be instructed when to do so.
- Make sure your handwriting is legible when you transfer your answers to the answer sheet.

POSSIBLE TASKS
conversations at home or between friends, radio announcements, parts of talks, conversations in shops, recorded messages, interviews with questions from a radio presenter

1 Look back at Parts 1 – 4. In your own words explain what you have to do in each Part.

	I have practised this and can do it!
In **Listening Part 1** I have to….	☐ ☐
In **Listening Part 2** I have to….	☐ ☐
In **Listening Part 3** I have to….	☐ ☐
In **Listening Part 4** I have to….	☐ ☐

86

2 Read the important points below and add ONE more of your own for each Part.

Perfect Part 1 – *pages 62-67*
- Look at the illustrations carefully and think of possible words you will hear in the listening.
- Listen for the gist of each conversation and choose the answer that best answer.
- _____

Perfect Part 2 – *pages 68-73*
- Underline the key words from each question so you know what kind of information you can expect.
- Use the second listening to make sure your answers are correct.
- _____

Perfect Part 3 – *pages 74-79*
- Read and listen to the instructions very carefully. Try to predict the kind of information the goes in each gap.
- The information might be: places, events, people talking about courses, holidays or trips.
- _____

Perfect Part 4 – *pages 80-85*
- Listen to the instructions carefully. Use the pause to read the question and think of the context.
- Focus on detailed understanding of the text, and then try to answer the questions the first time you listen.
- _____

Now you'll be perfect!!

1 Speaking

STEP 1 PREPARE

Can you tell me about yourself?

1 Match the picture with the activity.

> **WHAT YOU HAVE TO DO**
>
> In this part:
> - you will be asked questions about yourself, your daily routine, your likes and dislikes, and you may be asked about your plans for the future.
> - You will be examined with another candidate, sometimes even two other candidates. There will be two examiners in the room. You will only speak directly to one of them.

- playing the guitar
- chatting to friends on the phone
- playing video games
- travelling
- shopping
- studying
- going to the cinema
- riding a bicycle
- playing sports

> **Useful Language for Part 1!**
>
> **Vocabulary to describe things familiar to you** such as your school, your house.
> **Vocabulary to describe your likes and dislikes**
> **Expressions to talk about your past, your present circumstances, and future plans**.e.g.: last year I went to school in Taiwan, next year I'm going to Norway on holiday.
> **Greetings:** e.g. Hello, I'm Nils.

2 Work in groups. Ask your classmates what they like to do in their free time.

What do you do when you're not studying?

I really love music. I sing and play the cello, so I spend a lot of time with my choir and orchestra. What about you?

I like sport more than music, but when I'm running I use the time to listen to music and audiobooks.

Speaking 1

3 Match the examiner's questions to the student's answers.

1 What's your name?
2 How old are you?
3 Where do you come from?
4 Do you study English at school?
5 Tell us about your English teacher.
6 What's your favourite school subject?
7 What do you enjoy doing in your free time?
8 Tell us about your family.
9 What do you want to do when you are older?
10 What did you do last weekend?

a I enjoy listening to music and playing computer games.
b I like music best because we don't have a lot of studying to do!
c I'm from Gdansk in Poland. It's a big city by the sea.
d I went out with my friends and did my homework for school.
e I'd like to be a teacher and work with young children.
f My English teacher is very nice and helpful. We learn a lot in her lessons. She's from London.
g My name's Marek Boloski.
h There are four people in my family – my parents, my sister and myself. We all get on very well together.
i I'm 13 years old.
j Yes, I do. We have three hours a week.

4 In pairs, find out the following information about your partner. Make a note of the questions you use and hear.

Information I need	Questions	About my partner
name		
age		
nationality		
place of residence		
school		
family		
future plans		
free time		
last holiday		
worst school subject		

5 What about you? Introduce yourself to the class and tell them as much about yourself as possible. Answer any additional questions they ask.

1 Speaking

STEP 2 PRACTISE

1 Match the two halves of each question and then ask your partner.

1	What	a	do you get to school everyday?
2	Where	b	tell us about your favourite teacher?
3	What is	c	about your English class.
4	Tell us	d	got a favourite subject at school?
5	Can you	e	do you live?
6	Would	f	you like to learn to play a musical instrument?
7	Have you	g	your favourite day of the week? Why?
8	How	h	do you like doing after school?

2 Put the names of the people involved in the speaking test in the correct place and describe what their roles are.

Person	Role
the interlocutor	
the assessor	
the candidates	

1 _____
2 _____
3 _____

3 Put the words from the following questions in the correct order and answer them.

1 your / us / family / Tell / about
2 the morning / or / do / like / best, / What / you / the afternoon?
3 do / mobile phone? / How / you / use / a / often
4 How / get / you / do / to / every day / school?
5 do / What / doing / enjoy / you / time? / free / your / in
6 like / us / about / teacher / a / you / Tell
7 favourite / subject? / What's school / your

Speaking 1

4 Read the conversation below. Decide which question from the last exercise the teacher asked Maria.

Teacher: 1 _____

Maria: So, I really like my English teacher, because she makes us feel part of the lesson. She helps us understand difficult concepts and the classes are fun.

Teacher: 2 _____

Maria: I use it every day. I normally use it to chat to my friends, and sometimes to watch videos and listen to music.

Teacher: 3 _____

Maria: I take the bus near my house, and the underground. It takes me about an hour to get to school.

Teacher: 4 _____

Maria: The morning because I'm a morning person. I like having breakfast with my family, and going to school.

Teacher: 5 _____

Maria: I really like languages, history, and maths but I also enjoy music and art.

Teacher: 6 _____

Maria: I have a big family. There are six people in my family. Of course, I have my parents, then I have one brother and two sisters. My oldest brother is 23 years old and my youngest sister is 8 years old.

Teacher: 7 _____

Maria: I usually watch TV, and sometimes I read books or listen to music.

5 Read the conversation below. Decide which question from Exercise 4 the teacher asked Maria. Mark the following statements true or false.

1 Maria likes her English teacher because the classes are fun, and she helps her students. T ☐ F ☐
2 Maria doesn't like to use her mobile phone. She prefers to listen to music. T ☐ F ☐
3 María takes the underground to go to school. She lives very near. T ☐ F ☐
4 Maria is a morning person. She enjoys spending the morning with her family. T ☐ F ☐
5 Maria likes many school subjects including maths and music. T ☐ F ☐
6 María has one older brother who is twenty-five years old. T ☐ F ☐
7 María watches TV and listens to music in her free time. T ☐ F ☐

1 Speaking

STEP 3 PASS

> **EXAM TIP!**
> - Don't worry if you don't understand a question. You can ask the interlocutor to repeat it.
> - Try to practise talking about your home life, your school life, and your likes and dislikes as much as you can.

PHASE 1

Interlocutor

To A/B: Good morning / afternoon / evening
Can I have your mark sheets please?

To A/B I'm _____ and this is _____.

To A What's your name? How old are you?
Thank you.

To B What's your name? How old are you?
Thank you.

To B Where do you live? Who do you live with?
Thank you.

To A Where do you live? Who do you live with?
Thank you.

Speaking 1

> **EXAM TIP!**
> - Try not to give short answers in phase 2 questions. Always try to expand by giving examples and if possible, talking about your experiences.

PHASE 2

Interlocutor

(The interlocutor may ask one or more of the following questions.)

Tell us about your favourite teacher.

What's your favourite subject at school?

What do you like doing at weekends?

Tell us about the town where you live.

What did you do last weekend?

What do you enjoy doing in your free time?

What do you usually eat for lunch?

What are your plans for this evening?

Tell us about what you enjoy doing with your friends or family.

Describe a normal day at your school.

Tell us about your last holiday.

What is your favourite time of the day?

2 Speaking

STEP 1 PREPARE

What can you see?

WHAT YOU HAVE TO DO

In this part:
- you have to describe a photograph using appropriate vocabulary.
- you are assessed on how well you can use the language in your description.

1 Look at the photos.
- What are the people doing?
- Do you think they are having a good time?
- Describe them to your partner. Think about how they look and feel as well as what they are wearing and what they are doing.

2 Look at the photo and read how a student, Trudi, described it. Look at the underlined mistakes she made and correct them. You may need to add some words.

In the photograph there **1** <u>is</u> two children playing football with **2** <u>his</u> family in the park. They are enjoying **3** <u>himself</u> and having a good time. The weather seems nice and sunny. They aren't **4** <u>wear</u> shoes. In the background I can see many trees and some **5** <u>flower</u>. This park seems like a very nice place **6** <u>for</u> play games because the family is having a good time.

1 _____
2 _____
3 _____
4 _____
5 _____
6 _____

Useful Language for Part 2!

- Phrases to describe photographs such as: In this picture you can see…, In the middle of the picture etc.
- "There is" to talk about singular things in the photographs, and "there are " for plural.

Speaking 2

3 Match these words with picture A or B.

A

B

1 watch
2 jogging
3 health
4 celebration
5 match
6 goal
7 trainers
8 workout
9 outdoors
10 champion

4 In pairs, think of at least one adverb or adjective that you can use to describe the words from Exercise 3.

	adjective or adverb 1	adjective or adverb 2
watch		
jogging		
health		
celebration		
match		
goal		
trainers		
workout		

5 Describe the photo to your partner. Think about:

- who they are
- what they are doing
- where they are
- what's in the background
- where they might be going

95

2 Speaking

STEP 2 PRACTISE

1 Look at the photo of a family celebrating a special occasion together. Answer the questions.

1 Where are the family?
2 What are they doing?
3 Describe the people you can see – their clothes, their general appearance, and how they are feeling.
4 Describe what else you can see in the photo.

2 Look at the photo of a group of friends studying together. Answer the questions.

1 Where are the friends?
2 What are they doing?
3 Describe the people you can see – their clothes, their general appearance, how they are feeling.
4 Describe what else you can see in the photo.

3 Look at the exam task on page 97 that the interlocutor has just given you. Before you answer the questions, make some notes.

people	
feelings	
clothes	
before	
now	
after	

Speaking 2

Candidate A *approx. 1 minute*

Candidate B *approx. 1 minute*

4 ▶ **Now describe the picture to your partner. If you are the person listening, give your partner some ideas about what they could do better.**

2 Speaking

STEP 3 PASS

EXAM TIP!
- If you don't know a word, it's ok. Try to describe the word using words you know.
- Remember to describe more than just what you can see – include feelings.

Interlocutor: Now I'd like each of you to talk on your own about something. I'm going to give each of you a photograph and I'd like you to talk about it. **A**, here is your photograph. It shows **people learning something new.**

B, you just listen.

A, please tell us what you can see in the photograph.

Candidate A *approx. 1 minute*

Speaking 2

> **EXAM TIP!**
> - Mention what happened before the picture as well as what might be about to happen.
> - If there are several people in the picture, make sure you describe them all.

Interlocutor B, here is your photograph. It shows **people doing sport**

A, you just listen.

B, please tell us what you can see in the photograph.

Candidate B *approx. 1 minute*

3 Speaking

STEP 1 PREPARE

What should we do?

WHAT YOU HAVE TO DO

In this part:
- You have to talk to the other candidate about a situation that is not real.
- You need to look at the pictures and talk to each other about what you see.

1 Look at the pictures. What can you see?

2 Write the name of the place in the table and think of at least three advantages and disadvantages of shopping in these places.

Place	Advantages	Disadvantages
1.		
2.		
3.		
4.		
5.		

Useful Language for Part 3!

Phrases for asking for and giving opinions e.g. What do you think about…? I'm not sure about that.
Phrases for agreeing and disagreeing e.g. Yes, that's a great idea. Maybe, but we could also…
Phrases for making suggestions e.g. Why don't we…? How about ….?
Phrases for discussing alternatives e.g. What if we ….? Instead of …., we could ….

3 Your friends want to buy a new T-shirt. In pairs, talk about the different places in the pictures and decide which one would be the best option.

4 Trish and Tom are trying to decide what to buy their friend, Sam, for his birthday. Read the text and complete the conversation with these words. If more than one word is possible, choose the one you think fits best.

Possible presents for Sam:
T-shirt
book
football
computer game

about *(x2)*   can   could *(x2)*
for   if   might *(x3)*   on   shall
sure   would

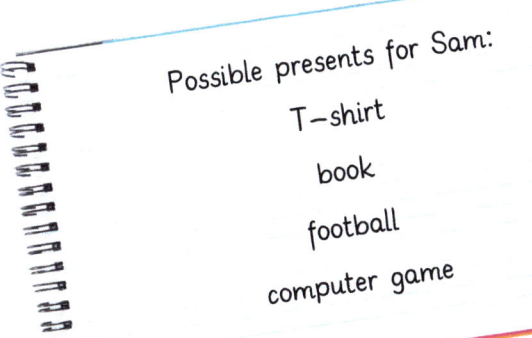

Trish: So, Tom, what 1 _____ we buy for Sam's birthday? A football 2 _____ be a good idea.

Tom: Yes, he's really keen 3 _____ the game, but he's probably got a football already. Let's think 4 _____ the other ideas as well. A computer game 5 _____ be a bit expensive, I think.

Trish: I agree. I don't think we 6 _____ afford that. How 7 _____ a book? Does he read much?

Tom: I don't know. We 8 _____ get him a book about his favourite footballer – that 9 _____ be a good present. What do you think?

Trish: Yes, that's possible. But T-shirts are always useful and I've seen some nice ones with a picture of a footballer on the front.

Tom: I'm not 10 _____ about a T-shirt; he 11 _____ not like it.

Trish: Well, he 12 _____ always change it if he doesn't. Shall we decide on that?

Tom: OK then, let's look 13 _____ a T-shirt. 14 _____ we don't find anything suitable, then we can get him a book.

Trish: That's a good idea, let's do that.

3 Speaking

STEP 2 PRACTISE

1 **Discuss these questions with your partner.**
- If somebody comes to visit you, where do you usually take them?
- And why?
- Is there anywhere you wouldn't take them?
- Why?

2 **Read the situation below, look at the pictures and discuss them. When you have finished, tell the rest of the class about what you have decided.**

Penfriend to stay

Bella

Bella's penfriend, Ina, is coming to stay with her for a week. Talk together about the different things the two girls could do and decide which would be the most interesting.

Remember to think about the different aspects and say why you think something. Make sure you discuss these points. Add two more of your own.

Ina

- What does each girl like and not like doing?
- What have they got in common?
- Has the visitor been here before?
- What clothes will she have with her?

- _____
- _____

Useful phrases

Well firstly, they could …
Do you think that a(n) … would be interesting?
I think it would be a good idea to …
They might like to …
I'm not sure about the …
Do you think they would enjoy …?
So, we think the most interesting activity would be …

Speaking 3

3 Look at the profiles and preferences of these two boys. They are staying with you and your family and want to have an amazing weekend. Work with a partner and plan the weekend for them.

	Nanouk	Jean-Luc
Profile	14, French, Lyon	13, Belgian, Brussels
Likes	• swimming • rap music • hiking	• environmental issues • history • watching films
Dislikes	• going to the cinema • cycling • horses	• all kinds of sports • eating meat • beaches

4 Present your plan to another group.

- Discuss why your suggestions are better than theirs.
- Find points that are bad about their suggestions.
- Find points that are good about their suggestions.
- Try to reach an agreement about whose plan is better.

3 Speaking

STEP 3 PASS

EXAM TIP!
- Try to say as much as you can about each photo before you make the final decision.
- Don't worry if the examiner interrupts you. If they do, it's because you have used up the time for the task.

PASS A

Interlocutor:

A boy is going on a long train journey with his parents. He wants to take something with him to do on the train. Talk together about the different things he could take and then decide which would be most interesting for him to do.

Speaking 3

> **EXAM TIP!**
> - Remember that the conversation with the other candidate should be for about 2-3 minutes.
> - Try to compromise with the other candidate so that you can reach a final decision. You don't necessarily need to believe what you are saying!

PASS B

A family is looking for different things to do at the weekend. Talk about the different things they could do and decide with activity would be most fun.

105

4 Speaking

STEP 1 PREPARE

What do you like doing?

WHAT YOU HAVE TO DO

In this part:
- You will talk about your likes and dislikes, preferences and opinions.
- The content of this part is linked to Part 3.
- You may have to answer questions the examiner asks you or discuss something with the other candidate(s).

1 Look at the pictures and talk to your partner.
- What are the people doing?
- Where are they?
- Do you do any of these things with your friends?
- What else do you like doing with your friends?

2 Make a list of things you like and don't like doing. Rank them based on how much you like / don't like them and give at least one reason.

Things I like doing with my friends	Things I don't like doing with my friends
1. _____ because _____ .	1. _____ because _____ .
2. _____ because _____ .	2. _____ because _____ .
3. _____ because _____ .	3. _____ because _____ .
4. _____ because _____ .	4. _____ because _____ .
5. _____ because _____ .	5. _____ because _____ .

Speaking 4

3 Complete the expressions you can use to give your opinion with the words from the box. Use each phrase only once.

- convinced
- opinion
- people
- feeling
- agree
- seems
- think
- would
- mean

What I _____ is ….

Do you _____?

In my _____ we should…

What do you _____?

My _____ is that….

I'm not so _____ that…

It _____ to me that….

Some _____ say that…

That _____ be a good idea.

4 Talk to people in your class. Use the phrases to discuss your preferences and why you like or dislike them so much. Try and find someone who has the same preferences as you.

5 Jen and Sophie both love hiking. Discuss these questions with your partner.

Where do you like hiking?
- When was the last time you went hiking?
- Do you prefer going on short hikes or long hikes?
- Do you prefer to go hiking with your friends or family?
- Do you think hiking is the best way to exercise?

6 Tell me about the last time you…. Choose four cards and ask your partner the questions.

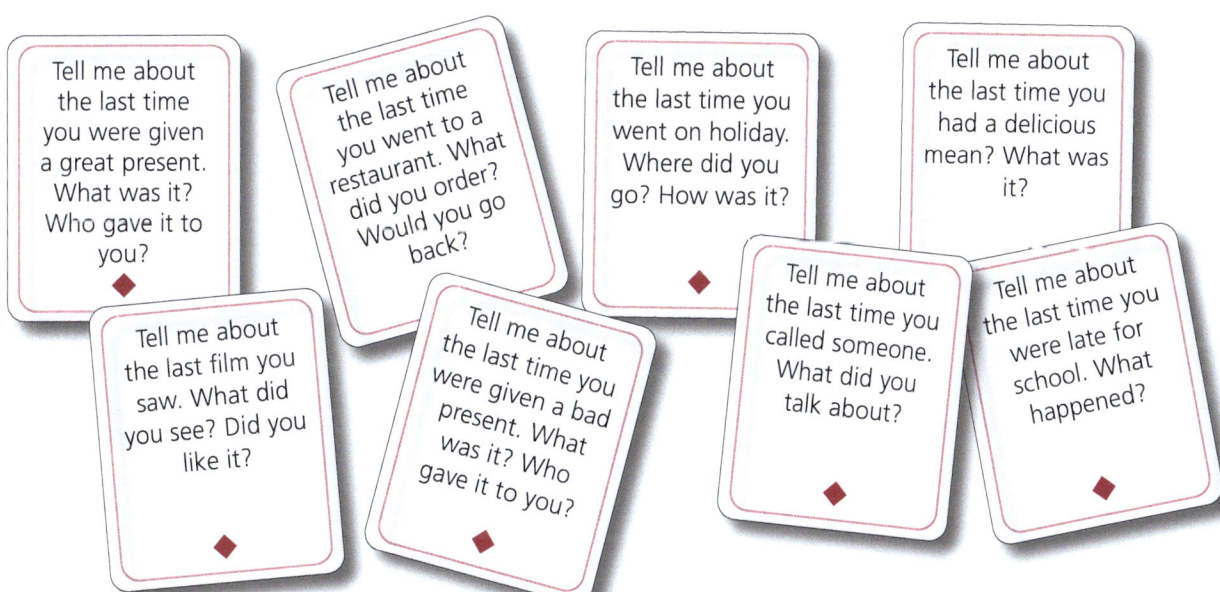

107

4 Speaking

STEP 2 PRACTISE

1 Look at the picture below. Think about the people you see. Think of some questions the examiner could ask about them.

friends

2 Talk about the following questions with your partner. Use the phrases in the box to help you.

- how about you?
- in my opinion
- I don't know if I agree with
- that sounds amazing
- do you agree?
- what do you think?

- Do you prefer to spend time with your friends or with your family?
- What activities do you normally do with your friends?
- Do you think it's better to text your friends or to speak to them face to face? Why?
- Do you think technology helps you keep in touch with your friends? How?
- Do you think that young people spend too much time with their friends?

Useful Language for Part 4!

Turn-taking language e.g.: What about you? How about you? What do you think about…?
Phrases to give your opinion about things e.g.: "I believe that.." "I think that…"

Speaking 4

3 Talk about the following questions with your partner. Use the phrases in the box to help you.

- don't you think …?
- I really think
- I'm not so sure about that
- sounds great, but …
- don't you agree?
- what about you?

school

- Do you prefer to go to school on foot or by public transport?
- What are your favourite subjects at school? And your worst subjects?
- Do you think it's better to do your homework as soon as you get it or save it for the weekend?
- Do you think technology is used well in your classroom? And for learning outside the classroom?
- Do you think that young people spend too much time at school and doing homework?

food and drink
sport   places
the environment
clothes   fitness
weather   holidays
jobs

4 Choose a topic from the jar. Using the examples in Tasks 2 and 3, make a note of five questions you think the examiner could ask. Then ask your partner the questions. You can do this with as many topics as you like!

109

4 Speaking

STEP 3 PASS

> **EXAM TIP!**
> - It's very important that you respond to what the examiner or your partner says to keep the conversation going.
> - Remember to give reasons for your opinions.

PASS A

- Have you ever travelled by plane? – (How was the experience?)

- Do you prefer to travel by plane or by train? (why)

- Do you prefer to go to school by car or by bus?

- Do you use public transport?

- Do you think it's important to find environmentally-friendly alternatives to how we currently travel?

Speaking 4

> **EXAM TIP!**
> - Avoid very short answers. You might find it helpful to use a word like "and" after you agree of disagree. This will automatically make you add more information.
> - Don't worry about making mistakes! And if you don't have your own opinion on something you are asked, just make something up!

PASS B

- What kind of places do you enjoy visiting?

- What place would you recommend that people should visit in your city?

- Talk about the last place you visited with your family.

- What city would you most like to visit with your family?

- Do you go to the same places with your friends and with your family?

Speaking

PERFECT!

What's in the Speaking exam?

4 Speaking Parts

How long does it last?

12 to **17** minutes

What do you have to learn before the exam?

- To answer questions about yourself
- To describe a photograph
- To make and respond to suggestions
- To discuss likes, dislikes, opinions, habits etc.

In the exam:

- Arrive at the exam venue with plenty of time to spare.
- If you don't understand instructions, it's OK to ask the examiner to repeat them.
- Don't learn set answers for this part. They don't sound natural, and they probably won't answer the question.

family
likes   friends   home
school   free time   food
health   sport   hobbies   feelings
dislikes   places   shopping
nature   travel

1 Look back at Parts 1 – 4. In your own words explain what you have to do in each Part.

I have practised this and can do it!

In **Speaking Part 1** I have to….

☐
☐

In **Speaking Part 2** I have to….

☐
☐

In **Speaking Part 3** I have to….

☐
☐

In **Speaking Part 4** I have to….

☐
☐

Speaking

2 Read the important points below and add ONE more of your own for each Part.

Perfect Part 1 – *pages 88-93*

- It's normal to feel nervous in this part of the test – but don't worry. This part focuses on every day, simple language, and it's designed to settle you into the test.
- Listen carefully to the questions and give appropriate answers.

- _____
  _____
  _____

Perfect Part 2 – *pages 94-99*

- Keep your descriptions simple, and don't talk about the wider issues represented in the photographs.
- Describe the photographs as fully as possible. Imagine you're describing the photograph to a person who can't see it.

- _____
  _____

Perfect Part 3 – *pages 100-105*

- Try to participate and encourage your partner to participate. In this part you're assessed on using the appropriate language and interactive strategies.
- Don't stop talking until the interlocutor stops you. If this happens it means you've used the allocated time. Remember you're not assessed on completing the task.

- _____
  _____

Perfect Part 4 – *pages 106-111*

- Listen carefully to the questions and give relevant answers. Remember that after your partner has been asked a question, they might ask you the same question, or for your opinion.
- You may be required to answer your questions individually or to interact with your partner.

- _____
  _____

Now you'll be perfect!!

Reading Part 1

Questions 1-5

For each question, choose the correct answer.

FOR RENT Lovely 1-bedroom flat with large living room and separate kitchen. Close to shops. £400 per month, electricity and water included

1

A The price of the bills for electricity and water is £400 per month.

B You don't pay extra for electricity and water.

C You must pay extra if you want electricity and water.

How to cook

1. Place pasta in a saucepan of boiling water. Add a teaspoon of salt.
2. Boil for no longer than 10 minutes.
3. When pasta is cooked, remove from the pan immediately. Serve with fresh tomato sauce.

2

The cooking instructions say you should

A add salt when you have cooked the pasta.

B cook the pasta in the tomato sauce.

C time the cooking of the pasta carefully.

3

A You only have to pay £35 for your first time at the gym.

B You don't have to pay anything for your first time at the gym.

C You don't need to pay anything at the gym until the 12th of March.

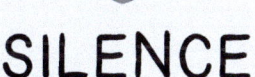

4

A You mustn't make any noise outside this room.

B You must only enter if you have an exam.

C You mustn't go inside with your English books.

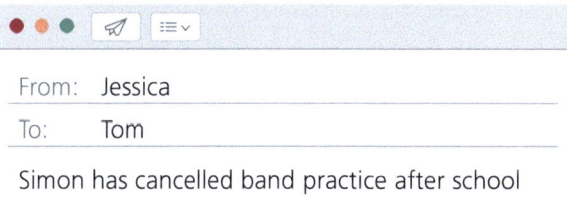

5

Why has Jessica written the email?

A to see if Tom is going to band practice

B to tell Tom why she can't come to band practice

C to inform Tom about the new time for band practice

Reading Part 2

Questions 6 – 10

For each question, choose the correct answer.

The teenagers below are all looking for an activity they can do to help the environment.
On the opposite page there are descriptions of eight environmentally-friendly activity ideas.
Decide which activity would be the most suitable for the teenagers below.

6

James knows lots about the environment and would like to share his advice and tips for helping the environment. He would also like to inform people of the different projects that are going on in the local neighbourhood.

7

Maria is interested in helping out in the area where she lives. She hasn't got a lot of free time, but she would like to get outside more. She likes places to be clean and neat.

8

Ivan is keen on making and building things and wants to become an artist. He would like to do something where he can be creative and not waste any old unwanted items.

9

Gemma is looking for an event she can organise at school with her classmates. She enjoys being active, and would like to do something outside that involves sport.

10

Katie is really interested in animals. She would like to do something with a bit of land at school that would help local wildlife and that everyone at school would enjoy.

Environmentally-friendly activities for teens

A The local park clean-up happens once a year and it really improves your neighbourhood. You only have to give a few hours of your time and you can make a huge difference to other people's lives. Picking up rubbish, clearing pathways and cleaning up leaves are just some of the useful things you will do.

B If you have got lots of time to spare, then why not make a vegetable garden? Growing your own vegetables is a lot healthier and cheaper than buying food from the supermarket. You don't need a large field, just a small area in your garden. Or you can grow some vegetables in pots on your balcony.

C A great way to help a charity and to also do something to help the environment is to organise a walk or run. You could get a big group of your classmates together, design a route to run and then get family and people you know to give you money for the distance you run. You can then send this money to an environmental organisation.

D We throw away a huge amount of rubbish every year, but many of these objects can be used again. You could make a sculpture out of recycled material or even your own furniture, such as chairs and tables, from old metal or wood.

E Planting new trees is as important as saving the old ones. Choose a place that is sunny and has lots of space, then put your tree in the ground and watch it grow. This is a great activity to do at school too. Organise a tree-planting event with your teacher and classmates.

F Writing a blog about ideas for looking after the environment can be a fantastic way to tell others about different issues that interest you. You don't need any special equipment; there are lots of useful websites that can help you set up your own blog.

G Did you know supermarket plastic bags can last for nearly 500 years buried in the ground? They often end up as litter and can also harm wildlife. Why not design and make your own paper bags, then sell them to friends, family and people in your local neighbourhood?

H Set up a wildlife area at school. Animals and insects need somewhere safe to go and eat. Whether you've got lots of space or just a small corner, wildlife areas are a great way to help the environment. You can build a small pond, make a bird table or create a small animal rescue home.

Reading Part 3

Questions 11–15

For each question, choose the correct answer.

Lucia Manelli – architect

Lucia Manelli is a successful architect and has taken part in many projects in different parts of the world. She often thinks back to how it all began when she was a student at school.

It all started with a project about town planning. Lucia and her classmates were split into groups and were given a large sheet of blank paper on which to plan and create a new town. To start with, some of her classmates thought it was all a bit of a joke. Lucia, though, was never satisfied unless she tried her best. Her first thought was about a video game she'd played where they had built whole towns and cities. Some of that experience might be useful but she'd keep quiet about it. Most of the other students in the group had been abroad and had seen other cities.

Their teacher gave them the names of certain buildings to include on the map but was not willing to give any further help. The group with the best town map would win a trip to an exhibition of modern architecture. 'By the time a few days had passed,' Lucia says, 'I remember getting really excited about this project. I had thought of some excellent ways to improve the quality of people's lives and to create more open green spaces.' However, Lucia found the other classmates in her group a bit difficult to work with.

'The problem was,' she continues, 'that I wanted my ideas to be accepted by the rest of the group but everyone else felt differently. One person wanted a shopping centre opposite the school but I wanted a park; another person wanted a statue in the square but I wanted a fountain, and so on. It was hopeless!' Because of this, their town map was not great and another group won the prize. Strangely enough, it was for a plan of a green city – Lucia's idea all along!

However, Lucia soon started doing more projects, finding out about and comparing different styles of buildings for the 21st century. 'I'd never thought of becoming an architect because I had never shown much talent at drawing at school. Then later on, my parents sent me to some special drawing classes and somehow, something clicked and I started to produce some reasonable work.'

Since then, she has never looked back.

11 What were Lucia's first thoughts about getting ideas for the project?

    A She felt depressed that she hadn't travelled as much as the other students.

    B She was embarrassed about using ideas from a video game.

    C She was keen to tell the rest of the group about the video game.

    D She thought her classmates' attitude was very amusing.

12 How did Lucia feel about the class project after a few days?

    A She didn't find it challenging enough.

    B She was disappointed in the lack of help from the teacher.

    C She was satisfied with the way her group worked together.

    D She was very confident about her own ideas.

13 Why did Lucia's group not win the prize at school?

    A They didn't know enough about modern architectural styles.

    B They were not very good at designing buildings.

    C They were unable to agree on certain basic decisions.

    D They didn't have as good ideas as the other groups.

14 Lucia eventually decided to become an architect because

    A her drawing skills improved a lot.

    B she did a lot of research in that area.

    C her parents were in the same business.

    D her teacher encouraged her.

15 What would the writer say about Lucia?

    A She always did well at school and she didn't have to do any extra work at home. She always knew what job she wanted to do.

    B She put a lot of effort into finding out more about what interested her. She thought that her opinions were usually the best.

    C She was really popular with teachers and students, but her parents didn't support her in her choice of career.

    D She didn't want to work hard in subjects that didn't interest her, but she wanted her friends and teachers to like her.

Reading Part 4

Questions 16-20

Five sentences have been removed from the text below. For each question, choose the correct answer.

There are three extra sentences which you do not need to use.

A school with a difference!

A while ago, there was a fantastic documentary series on television about an orangutan school in the jungles of Borneo. And the funny thing was, the education of the orangutans – whose parents had gone missing – was organised into a nursery for babies, a forest school and an island university! **16** _____

The orang-utans are looked after by a specialised team who feed the babies but who also teach the older ones to start feeding themselves. **17** _____ For example, there was the lesson about how to break open a coconut to drink the milk inside. Several young orangutans couldn't do that and they got very annoyed with the whole thing!

Of course, as in any social group, the orangutans have to learn to get on with each other. There are the usual arguments over food, instances of bullying, and screams when one orangutan doesn't get what he or she wants. However, over time they learn to accept each other.

In one episode, the programme showed a lesson where the trainers from the school were teaching young orangutans to climb trees. This is an essential skill they need to learn. **18** _____ It took him a long time to get the courage to climb up and swing from a branch but when he eventually did it, he was so pleased with himself!

The whole aim of this 'education system' is to train the orangutans to be able to exist in the wild again and look after themselves. **19** _____

After the older orangutans are set free into the forest, there is no further contact with the people from the school. They now have to live as wild orangutans again and be accepted by the other orangutans who are already there.

The day when they say goodbye is a difficult one. **20** _____ They have successfully taught a young orangutan how to live in the wild again – where he belongs.

A There are often problems in the beginning.

B They won't have to stay at school forever!

C The number of orangutans became too big for the school.

D One of them in particular was really scared.

E Some of them try to escape and have to be brought back.

F However, the trainers are happy that their job is done.

G They show the same feelings that humans have.

H So the system, you could say, was similar to ours.

Practice Test

Reading Part 5

Questions 21–26

For each question, choose the correct answer.

Scuba diving at night

The first time you dive through the darkness of the ocean at night, you will see that it's a completely different world from during the day. It sounds a bit **(21)** _____ but if you follow certain rules, there's nothing to **(22)** _____ about. Always dive with a partner so you can have someone with you in an emergency. It's also a good **(23)** _____ to do the dive in the day first and check out the site. Finally, **(24)** _____ sure that your boat has got lights attached to it so you can find your way back after the dive!

Diving at night is best when the moon is bright since it lights up the water. However, divers **(25)** _____ take dive lights with them as well in order to see the colourful creatures coming out of their hiding places to feed. Bigger fish like sharks also use the darkness to go **(26)** _____ for their next meal. It's dinnertime in the ocean at night!

21	A	scary	B	frightened	C	nervous	D	terrified
22	A	mind	B	fear	C	worry	D	care
23	A	feeling	B	idea	C	thought	D	way
24	A	seem	B	do	C	keep	D	make
25	A	surely	B	absolutely	C	normally	D	unusually
26	A	attacking	B	hunting	C	swimming	D	eating

Reading Part 6

Questions 27–32

For each question, write the correct word. Write one word for each gap.

Hi Hannah,

Many thanks for your email. We have just come **1** _____ from our summer holiday where we had quite an adventure. We **2** _____ staying in a seaside village. My sister and I love horse–riding and **3** _____ was a farm nearby so my parents organised some lessons for us.

One day, as we were riding along a quiet road, my sister tried **4** _____ take a photo of us on her phone and she fell off! For about a minute, she couldn't breathe and I was very frightened! However, she soon felt better but her shoulder still hurt a lot. Later, we took her to the doctor who told her to rest it for a few days and **5** _____ do any more riding. So we lay on the beach for the rest of our holiday!

6 _____ don't we go horse-riding sometime? I think you'd like it!

Love,

Poppy

Writing Part 1

You **must** answer this question. Write your answer in about **100 words.**

Question 1
Read this email from your English friend Max and the notes you have made.

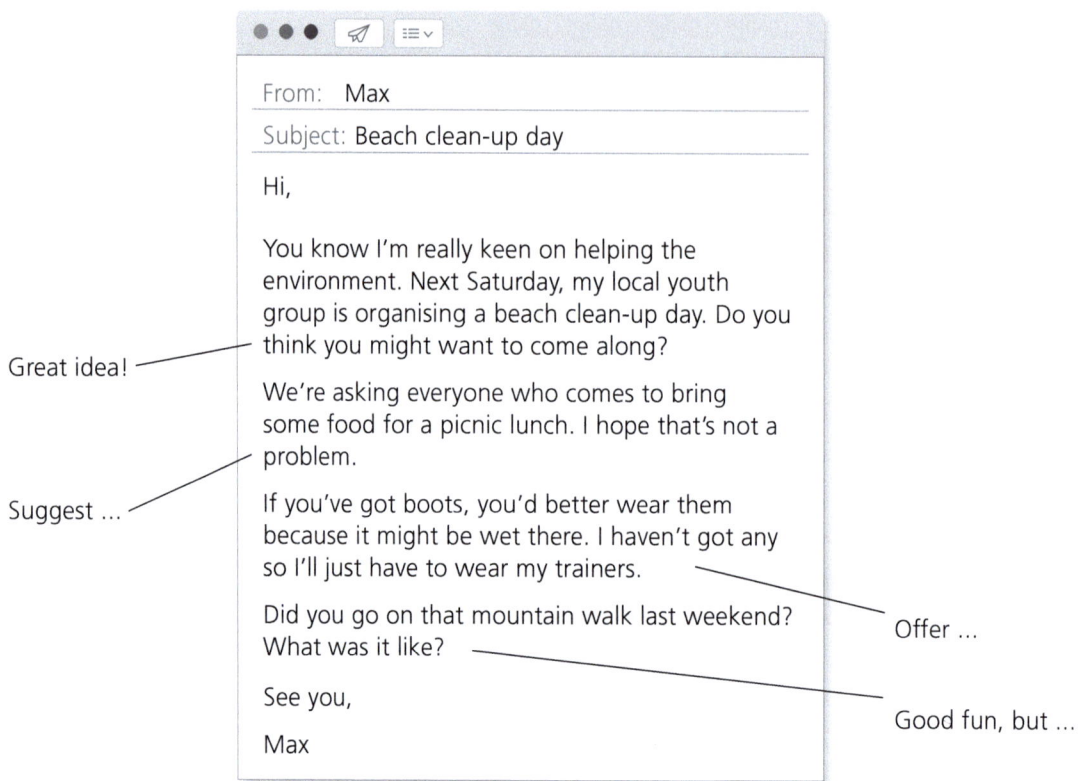

Write your **email**, using all the **notes**.

Writing Part 2

Choose **one** of these questions.
Write your answer in about **100 words**.

Question 2
You see this notice on an international English website for teenagers.

Articles wanted!
Films

Write an article about the films you watch. Do you like going to the cinema or watching films at home?

What type of films do you prefer? Why?

The best articles answering these questions will be published next month.

Write your **article**.

Question 3
Your English teacher has asked you to write a story. Your story must begin with this sentence:

Everything on our holiday last year went wrong from day one.

Write your **story**.

Practice Test

Listening PART 1

Questions 1-7

 For each question, choose the correct answer.

1 What will the weather be like tomorrow?

A

B

C

2 What type of accommodation will they probably stay in?

A

B

C

3 Which pet will the girl buy from the shop?

A

B

C

126

4 Why will the school be closed today?

A

B

C

5 What did Tara's mum buy?

A

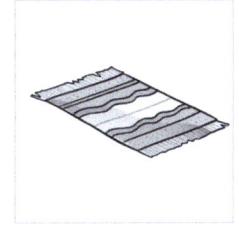
B

C

6 What instrument is the boy going to play?

A

B

C

7 Which role will Hannah have in the school play?

A

B

C

Listening PART 2

Questions 8-13

 For each question, choose the correct answer.

8 You will hear two friends talking about playing football. They agree

   A that football is fun to play.
   B that more women's football matches should be shown on television.
   C that more women should play football.

9 You will hear two friends talking about a party they are planning. The boy's mum:

   A is happy to have the party at her house.
   B is going to make the food and clear up afterwards.
   C doesn't know about the party yet.

10 You will hear a girl talk about a bad result she got. How does she feel about it?

   A disappointed
   B confident
   C annoyed

11 You will hear two friends talking about a film they went to. The girl thinks the acting was

   A terrible.
   B excellent.
   C amazing.

12 You will hear a boy talking about a play he's in. The play is at

   A 19:00.
   B 18:30.
   C 19:30.

13 You will hear two friends talking about an accident in the playground. The boy thinks Ms Johnson went to hospital

   A because of her headache.
   B because she lost a lot of blood.
   C because she had flu.

Listening PART 3

Questions 14-19

For each question, write the correct answer in the gap.
Write <u>one</u> or <u>two</u> words or a <u>number</u> or a <u>date</u> or a <u>time</u>.
You will hear some information about a young writers' summer camp.

SUMMER CAMP

Description: A summer camp for young writers who are interested in

(14) _____

Teaching style: fun and (15) _____

Classwork includes: coursework and (16) _____

Age groups

Lower age group: (17) _____

Upper age group: 15–16 years old.

Writing classes will teach students about: short stories,

(18) _____ writing, and writing play scripts for theatres.

After the course: parents will receive a (19) _____

Listening PART 4

Questions 20-25

 For each question, write the correct answer.
You will hear an interview with a girl called Chloe Connor who helps to protect the environment.

20 Why did the organisation "Help Our Planet" ask Chloe to join them?
   A People in the local neighbourhood recommended her work.
   B They liked the environmental work she was doing.
   C There was no one else as interested in the environment.

21 What does Chloe say about her work with the organisation?
   A She does it to earn credit at school.
   B She enjoys helping people.
   C She likes to plant new trees.

22 Chloe and the organisation recently built a garden on a piece of land to
   A improve the neighbourhood.
   B raise some money for charity.
   C inform people about the environment.

23 What does Chloe say about the problems with the environment?
   A If young people don't help, things will get worse.
   B Not many people care about the problems.
   C Older people should do more to help.

24 Chloe says teenagers can help the environment by
   A not using computers and other equipment.
   B going to more places on foot.
   C using public transport less.

25 According to Chloe, what are their plans for the future?
   A They will carry on their work and try and help other cities.
   B They aim to create their own website very soon.
   C They will try to get more people to join their organisation.

Practice Test

Speaking

Part 1 (2-3 minutes) Interlocutor:

Phase 1

Good morning / afternoon.

Could you tell me your name?

How old are you?

Where do you live?

Phase 2

Tell us about your favourite subject at school.

Where did you go for your last holiday?

Do you play on instrument?

Do you like going to the cinema?

Do you spend a lot of time online?

Tell us about your family.

What do you want to be when you are older?

Part 2 (3-5 minutes) Interlocutor:

I'd like you each to talk on your own about something. I'm going to give each of you a photograph of people singing or playing music.

Candidate A, here is your photograph. Please show it to Candidate B, but I'd like you to talk about it.

Candidate B, you just listen. I'll give you your photograph in a moment. Candidate A, please tell us what you can see in the photograph.

Now, Candidate B, here is your photograph. It shows people playing music in a band. Please show it to Candidate A and tell us what you can see in the picture.

Part 3 (4-5 minutes) Interlocutor:

I'm going to describe a situation to you.

A friend of yours is planning to get out of the city for a day and spend some time in the countryside. Talk together about things that you and your friend would need for a day trip to the countryside, and decide what would be the best things to take with you. Here is a picture with some ideas to help you.

Part 4 (3-4 minutes) Interlocutor:

What kinds of activities can you do in the countryside? And in the city?

Do you prefer trips to the countryside or going to cities? Why?

Where did you go on the last holiday you went on?

What's the best holiday you've ever been on?

Where do people from your country usually go on holiday?

Preparation Pack: Preliminary Grammar

What grammar do you need to know?

WHAT YOU HAVE TO DO
- You have to be able to talk about the present, past and future.
- You have to be able to use other structures and grammatical features expected at B1.

TALKING ABOUT...

The Present: present simple and present continuous

	Use the present simple…	Your examples
This exam **has** 4 papers.	to talk about facts and what is generally true.	
I **learn** five new English words every day.	to talk about habits (what always, often, sometimes, never happens).	
Felix **sits** down, **opens** his book and then **looks** at the pictures.	to talk about a series of events (e.g. in a story).	
Nina **loves** exams!	to talk about attitudes and feelings.	

	Use the present continuous…	Your examples
I**'m reading** this example sentence.	to talk about what is going on at the moment.	
The exam is in June. **Isa is studying** hard so she can get a good grade.	to talk about things that are happening for a short time.	

The Past: present simple and past continuous

	Use the past simple…	Your examples
I **did** all my homework on Friday afternoon.	to talk about completed activities or events in the past (often with dates, yesterday, last year, a year ago etc).	
It **was** my birthday yesterday, so I **got** up early and **helped** my Dad bake muffins, and then I **put** them in a box and **took** them to school.	to talk about a series of actions of events in the past (e.g. in a story).	

	Use the past continuous…	Your examples
Lenny **was** still **writing** his answer, when the teacher told us to stop.	to talk about the "background" to past events, or to say what was happening when another event happened.	
Jess **was reading** something on her tablet, Sam **was doing** his homework and the twins **were playing** a game.	to talk about several activities that were going on at the same time.	

	Use the present perfect…	Your examples
Alba **has been** at this school for three years.	to talk about something that started in the past, but is still happening (often with expressions of time such as always, all week, for and since etc).	
Have you ever **done** an exam like this before?	to talk about experiences in the past (often with expressions of time such as ever, yet, never, twice etc).	
The email with my exam results **has** just **come**!	to show that the result of a past activity is important (often with just).	

	Use the past perfect simple…	Your examples
Jack went to bed after he **had written** his essay.	to show which event happened first in the past. The past perfect simple is often used in the same sentence as the past simple.	

Some key irregular verbs

verb	past simple	past participle	verb	past simple	past participle
be	was/ were	been	go	went	gone
become	became	become	have	had	had
break	broke	broken	know	knew	known
bring	brought	brought	lose	lost	lost
buy	bought	bought	make	made	made
catch	caught	caught	run	ran	run
come	came	come	say	said	said
do	did	done	see	saw	seen
drink	drank	drunk	sit	sat	sat
eat	ate	eaten	sleep	slept	slept
fall	fell	fallen	stand	stood	stood
find	found	found	swim	swam	swum
fly	flew	flown	take	took	taken
get	got	got	wake	woke	woken
give	gave	given	write	wrote	written

This is only a selection of some of the irregular verbs in English. Find more verbs and check you know the past simple and past participle!

You can find a longer table of verbs here.

The Future

	Use the present simple…	Your examples
The exam **starts** at 9:00 on Thursday morning.	to talk about timetables.	
	Use the present continuous…	**Your examples**
We**'re having** a party after the exam!	to talk about fixed plans.	
	Use going to + infinitive …	**Your examples**
I**'m going to do** lots of practice tests to help me prepare for the exam.	to talk about plans and intentions.	
I find reading really easy, so I**'m** definitely **going to pass** those parts!	to talk about things that are almost certain to happen.	
	Use will + infinitive …	**Your examples**
We all studied hard, so I think we **will pass**.	to talk about predictions or things you think are likely to happen.	
I**'ll** probably **sleep** for a week after the exam!	to talk about promises and decisions you make as you speak.	

Preparation Pack: Preliminary Words

Words you need to talk about...

Words you need to talk about...

WHAT YOU HAVE TO DO
- In all parts of the exam you will need to be familiar with vocabulary related to topics.
- Make sure you know these words! It would be helpful to know even more, so add new words to the topic areas as you learn them.

CLOTHES AND ACCESSORIES

Describing clothes: short / long / dirty / old-fashioned / uncomfortable

Sport: swimsuit / swimming trunks / kit

Things you need every day: glasses / bag / purse / wallet / watch / phone / earphones / backpack

Winter: coat / scarf / gloves / hat / boots

Sunny: shorts / T-shirt / sunglasses / cap

School uniform: belt / shirt / trousers / skirt / tie / jacket / jumper

Smart clothes: suit / dress

Rain: raincoat / umbrella

Everyday clothes: jeans / socks / shoes / underwear

Jewellery: bracelet / earrings / necklace / ring

> You fasten your belt to make sure your trousers stay up.
> You put your school uniform on in the morning.
> Those blue shoes go well with your blue top.
> It's a good idea to try clothes on in the shop to make sure they fit.

COMMUNICATION AND TECHNOLOGY

Hardware: camera / smart/mobile phone / tablet / computer / keyboard / mouse / screen / CD / DVD player / webcam

Internet: online / website / web / net / web page / address / @ / password / dot

Actions: click / chat / connect / print

Communication: blog / email / letter / envelope / message / parcel / social media / text / vlog

Digital tools: video / download / upload / file

Preparation Pack: Preliminary Words

EDUCATION

Levels:
beginner / intermediate / advanced

People:
classmate / teacher / coach / student / pupil

Progress:
test / exam(ination)

School subjects:
art / economics / science: biology / chemistry / physics / geography / history / English / maths / mathematics

Adjectives:
clever / boring / interesting / difficult / easy

The classroom:
lesson / board / whiteboard / blackboard / desk / chair / chalk / pens / markers / ruler / rubber/eraser / dictionary / bell

Verbs:
know / learn / revise / remember / research / practise / do your homework / work on a project / write an essay

ENTERTAINMENT AND MEDIA

Theatre / film:
act / actor / cinema / stage / star / perform / play

Art:
cartoon / draw / drawing / sketch / exhibition / museum / artist

Writing:
article / book / author / advertisement (ad) / magazine

Games:
board game / chess

Equipment:
camera

Dance:
dancer / ballet / ballerina

Events:
festival / competition

Music:
classical / pop / rock / rap / hip hop / folk / opera / concert / instruments: drum, piano, violin, flute / musician / singer / band / orchestra / soundtrack

Television:
chat show / documentary / news / celebrity / drama / presenter / programme / quiz / soap opera

Genres:
adventure / action / drama / horror / comedy / thriller

COUNTRIES

Language:
Danish / Spanish / Chinese

Country:
Denmark / Peru / China

Nationality:
Danish / Peruvian / Chinese

Preparation Pack: Preliminary Words

HEALTH AND MEDICINE

People: doctor / nurse / patient / dentist

The body: back / blood / stomach / hand / finger / foot / leg / neck / heart / head / wrist / ankle / shoulder / chin

At the doctor's / hospital: ambulance / appointment / prescription

Exercise: jogging / gym / run / stretch / walk

Problems with the body: ill / pain / have a temperature / feel sick / flu

Symptoms: cough / sneeze / earache / stomach ache / bleed / sore throat

Accidents: fall / cut / hurt / break / emergency / damage / injure / recover

Medicine: aspirin / tablet / cough medicine / pharmacy

HOBBIES AND LEISURE

Places to go: beach / campsite / park / on a cruise / playground / sightseeing

Things to do: barbecue / camp / go camping / collect something e.g. stamps / dance / draw / go shopping / join a club / paint / have a picnic / do a quiz / play video games / hang out / sunbather

Things you can use: bike/bicycle / computer / tent / torch

HOUSE AND HOME

Things outside the house: balcony / gate / ladder / bush

Accommodation: flat / apartment / house / block of flats / property / upstairs / downstairs / rent

Rooms: bathroom / bedroom / dining room / entrance / hall / living room / sitting room

Things in the house: air-conditioning / bin / blanket / pillow / carpet / curtain / blinds / door / window / floor / roof / sink / shower / safe / toilet / bath / towel / basin / ceiling / heating

Furniture: armchair / sofa / bed / chair / bookcase / cupboard / desk

Adjectives: antique / modern

PLACES

To buy things: bookshop / department store / grocery store

To live or stay in: apartment block / cottage / prison / hotel / village / campsite

To learn: college / gallery / library / school / university

To eat and drink: café / restaurant

To visit in your free time: playground / zoo

In the countryside: field / forest / river / rainforest / stream / waterfall

By the sea: bay / cliff / harbour / port / seaside

To work: office / factory

To watch something: cinema / theatre / stadium

Preparation Pack: Preliminary Words

SPORT

Sport equipment: ball / bat / boat / racket / skateboard / surfboard / trainers

Places: pool / court / pitch / race track

Kinds of sport: athletics / badminton / baseball / basketball / cricket / cycling / extreme sports / fishing / golf / hockey / motor-racing / rugby / sailing / go skiing / yoga

People: athlete / champion / competitor / instructor

Equipment: boat / helmet / skateboard

Verbs: catch / climb / compete / hit / join in / score / take part / win a prize/medal

THE NATURAL WORLD

The environment: air / fire / ice / moon / sun / space / star / water / world / rainforest

Places: countryside / desert / cave / coast

People: explorer

Wildlife and vegetation: animal / bee / branch / dolphin / flower / frog / leaf / mosquito

Weather nouns: cloud / breeze / degrees / forecast / lightning / snow / storm / thunderstorm / wind

Directions: north / east / south / water

Seasons: spring / summer / autumn/fall / winter

Weather verbs: freeze / blow / get wet

Weather adjectives: cloudy / cold / foggy / hot / rainy / sunny / warm / wet / windy

TRAVEL AND TRANSPORT

Transport: (air)plane / ambulance / car / coach / ferry / helicopter / motorbike / scooter taxi / train / tram / bus / underground

Places: abroad / airport / embassy / motorway / platform / road / roundabout

Things you take: backpack / luggage / suitcase / guidebook / map

Reasons to travel: on business / on holiday/vacation

Travelling: delay / flight / journey / map / traffic / trip

Verbs: fly / land / miss the bus / move / return / stop / visit

People: driver / pilot / cabin crew / engineer / explorer / passenger / tour guide / tourist

At the airport: gate / boarding pass / passport / arrivals / departures / duty-free / immigration / visa

Preparation Pack: Preliminary Words

FOOD AND DRINK

Tastes: sweet / salty / bitter / delicious / disgusting / hot / spicy

Vegetables: carrot / potato / garlic / onion / peas / corn / mushroom / spinach

Meat: burger / beef / chicken / pork / lamb / bacon / ham

Poultry: chicken / duck / turkey

Fruit: apple / banana / orange / grapes / lemon / pear / strawberry / coconut

Containers: box / bottle / bowl

Meals: breakfast / snack / lunch / dinner / starter / main course / pudding / dessert

Way of cooking: boil / bake / break (an egg) / fry / grill

Sweet things: sweets / candy / biscuit / cake / honey / jam / sugar / chocolate

Fish: salmon / tuna
Dairy products: butter / milk / cheese / yoghurt / cream

Drinks: water / juice / lemonade / soft drinks / tea / coffee

Carbohydrates: bread / cereal / pasta / rice / toast / chips

Herbs and spices: chilli / salt / pepper

There are three courses on this menu.
This recipe is very complicated because there are so many ingredients.

FEELINGS, OPINIONS AND EXPERIENCES

Positive experience: awesome / amazing / fantastic / enjoyable

Negative experience: unpleasant / terrible / embarrassing / disappointing

Character: generous / nice / lovely / seriou[s]

Physical need: hungry / thirsty

Negative feeling: confused / jealous

Positive feeling: relieved / impressed

Appearance: beautiful / slim

WORK AND JOBS

Professions: architect / artist / businessman/woman / chemist / cleaner / cook / farmer / journalist / painter / photographer / police officer / receptionist / secretary / singer / waiter/waitress

Positions: boss / manager / customer / part time / full time

At work: break / canteen / contract / instructions / letter / meeting / staff / uniform

Leaving a job: quit / retire / resign

No job: out of work / unemployed

Getting a job: apply / candidate / career / interview / position / qualification / CV

Preparation Pack: Exam Checklist

Exam Checklist

Prepare for the exam. Here are some key points you need to think about before, during and at the end of the exam.

Tick ☑ the points below when you think are ready for the exam!

You need to take…
- 2 sharpened pencils
- 1 rubber

1 Before the exam

Revise topic vocabulary, grammar and useful phrases. ☐

Practise writing a short story or an email. Show it to your teacher or a friend. ☐

Make sure you know how much time you have for each paper. ☐

Do some practice exams in the time you are allowed. ☐

2 During the exam

When you do your practice exams, think about these points.

Answer each Part carefully but quickly. ☐

Check you have answered ALL the questions. ☐

Count the words in the Writing Paper. Make sure you have written the correct number. ☐

3 At the end of the exam

Carefully mark your answers on the Answer Sheet. ☐

Don't make any mistakes! If you do, rub it out and correct it. ☐

Write your answers in the Writing Paper directly on the Answer Sheet. ☐

Good luck and don't worry! You'll be brilliant!

You can't take…
- Your mobile phone.
- A dictionary.

Preparation Pack: Key Phrases

Useful phrases for Writing Parts 1 and 2

WRITING...

> **WHAT YOU HAVE TO DO**
> - In Writing Part 1 you have to write an email in response to a text.
> - In Writing Part 2 you have to write an article **or** a story.

An email (Writing Part 1)

Starting	**Informal:** Greeting: First sentence: **Semi-formal:** Greeting: First sentence:	Hi Jack, Hi, Thanks for your email. Good to hear from you. Sorry I haven't written recently. Dear Ms Potts Thank you for your email.
Making suggestions	Let's + infinitive without to, e.g.: Let's ask the other students what they think. How about + -ing, e.g.: How about setting up a club?	
Accepting an invitation	I'd love/I'd like + to + infinitive, e .g.: I'd love to go swimming with you. That would be nice. That's a great idea!	
Declining an invitation	I'm afraid I can't, because…. Maybe another time though. I'm really busy on Saturday. What about Sunday?	
Giving advice	Had better + infinitive without to, e.g.: We'd better ask for permission Why don't you check with your parents first?	
Talking about preferences	I love/like/hate + -ing, e.g.: I love organising other people. I'd rather + infinitive without to, e.g.: I'd rather play tennis than watch the football match.	
Ending	**Informal:** **Semi-formal:**	Bye, Bye for now, See you, See you soon Don't forget to write soon Best wishes, All the best I look forward to hearing from you again soon.

Preparation Pack: Key Phrases

An article (Writing Part 2)

Giving your opinion	In my opinion, e.g.: In my opinion, we should plant more trees. I think, e.g.: I think that there aren't enough areas for young people to go in our town. I believe, e.g.: I believe that everyone should join in and help.
Giving examples	For example, e.g.: We should all help to clean up the school. For example, we can pick up any litter and throw it in the bin. For instance, e.g.: There are lots of interesting things to do at weekends. For instance, there's a new ice-skating rink in the centre which is great fun.
Using connecting words	Because, e.g.: This is a good idea because many people will support it. Since, e.g.: Since life is more stressful these days, it's more important to take exercise. But, e.g.: It's important to be connected through the internet but we should have some time away from the computer.

A story (Writing Part 2)

Using past tenses	Past simple, e.g.: She left the house and ran down the road. Past continuous, e.g.: It was raining when he got off the bus. Past perfect, e.g.: I had forgotten my ticket and it was too late to go back and get it.
Using time phrases	At first, e.g.: At first, Sandy didn't know what to do. Then, e.g.: Then, she made her decision. Before, e.g.: Before getting on the bus, she rang her mother. After, e.g.: After that, things started to go wrong. Suddenly, e.g.: Suddenly, there was a loud noise and the bus stopped. When, e.g.: When the bus driver got off the bus, he told us what had happened.
Describing	**A situation** e.g.: There were a lot of people there. 　　It was an extremely hot day and David felt exhausted. **Feelings** e.g.: I was really frightened. She found the experience terrifying. I couldn't understand why people were laughing.

Useful phrases for Speaking Parts 1 + 2

SPEAKING...

> **WHAT YOU HAVE TO DO**
> - You have to be able to talk to and interact naturally with the examiner.
> - You have to give personal information in response to questions.
> - You have to describe a picture.

To the examiner

Introducing yourself	Name: Hi. / Good morning. I'm …. Age: I'm 13 years old. Where you are from: I was born in Singapore. Where you live: I live in Hong Kong.
Asking for clarification	I'm sorry / excuse me, I don't understand. Could you repeat the question, please? Could you say that again, please?
Winning time	Well, In fact,… Let me see / think about it for a second. I guess …

To describe a photograph

General introduction	In this picture you can see… It looks like the people in the photo are…. At the top / bottom of the picture there is.. In the middle of the picture I can see..
Talking about places	This seems to be a … They are in ….. The picture is set in ….
Describing people in a picture	The man/woman in the picture is wearing… The man/woman is probably a …. (name of a job) The man/woman in the picture seem to be about …. years old.
Making guesses	It might be… This thing could be ….

Preparation Pack: Key Phrases

To the other candidate(s)

Making suggestions	Let's How / what about …..ing? Why don't we…? Maybe we could….?
Giving your opinion	I think….because… I don't think….because… In my opinion, …
Asking for opinions	What do you think? What's your opinion on this? How do you feel about that? What about you?
Agreeing	You're right. That's (so) true. I think so too. I suppose so. That's how I feel. That's a good / great / fantastic idea. Agreed!
Disagreeing	I'm not sure about that. I don't know. Yes, but don't you think…? I completely disagree. Sorry, I think you're wrong.
Showing interest	Really? I see. Hmm. Yes.
Talking about likes and dislikes	I like / love I don't like / really don't like / can't stand I prefer *black phones* to *white phones*.
Changing the topic	Should we move on? How about if we talk about …. And what do you think about this….
Interrupting a conversation	Sorry for interrupting but…. Just a moment, I'd like to…. If I could just come in here. I think….

WHAT YOU HAVE TO DO

- You have to be able to talk to and interact naturally with the examiner.
- Make and respond to suggestions.
- Discuss likes and dislikes.

To talk about likes and dislikes

General likes and dislikes	I like/love/enjoy + gerund or noun I don't like / really dislike / hate + gerund or noun
Expressing preference	I would rather + infinitive I would prefer to …. I wouldn't like to …..

Photo Credits

123RF.com, Nidderau: 70 (mklrnt); Ingram Image, London: various; Shutterstock, New York: 6.1 (exopixel); 6.2 (kurhan); 108, 109.2 (Marina9); 47, 61, 87, 113, 137 (Treter); 8.1 (LDDesign); 54, 55 (venimo); 10.1 (Gajus); 71.1 (Hugo Felix); **Cover U1** (Panthep Boonsaree); 10.2, 11.1 (wavebreakmedia); various (Nosyrevy); 10.3, 62.4, 100.5 (Rawpixel.com); 10.4 (Studio KIWI); 10.5 (illpaxphotomatic); 11 (Tigger11th); 11.2 (antstang); 11.3 (FGC); 11.4 (rnl); 11.5 (Marian Fil); 11.6 (iodrakon); 11.7, 89.1 (szefei); 12.2 (karen roach); 12.3 (Alhovik); 12.4 (Gercen); 12.5 (StockAppeal); 13 (Elena3567); 14 (VikiVector); 15.1 (Alexandr III); 15.2 (invisible163); 16.1 (Ibooo7); 16.2 (Paper Wings); 16.3, 115 (Black creator 24); 16.4 (Vladimir Sviracevic); 16.5 (sattva78); 16.6 (Pavel K); 17 (Ninja Artist); 17 (RossHelen); 17.1 (Olena Zaskochenko); 17.2 (Asier Romero); 18.1, 109.1 (YanLev); 18.2, 28.2, 30.1 (Africa Studio); 18.3 (karelnoppe); 18.4 (lanych); 20.1 (goodluz); 20.2 (WAYHOME studio); 20.3 (Darren Baker); 20.4 (michaeljung); 20.5 (morrowlight); 23.1 (MilanMarkovic78); 24.1 (AJR_photo); 24.2 (fizkes); 24.3 (Roman Kosolapov); 25.1 (Luis Louro); 25.2 (jax10289); 25.3 (Sophie Leguil); 26.1, 103.1 (Ivonne Wierink); 26.2 (Michael Neil Thomas); 28.1, 38.1, 94.4, 96.1, 106.8 (Syda Productions); 28.3 (NataliTerr); 28.4 (Karlisz); 29.1 (FrimuFilms); 29.2, 69.3, 94.6 (Iakov Filimonov); 29.3 (Ahturner); 29.4 (siamionau pavel); 29.5 (Pinkcandy); 29.6 (Alla Ushakova); 29.7 (Olex Kmet); 29.8, 100.4 (Georgejmclittle); 29.9 (mikeledray); 31.2 (Ilya Osovetskiy); 32.2, 106.4, 106.6 (oliveromg); 34.1 (Irina Fischer); 34.2 (Tatiana Murr); 34.3 (Christo); 35.1 (atm2003); 35.2 (kavalenkava); 35.3 (Daniel Fung); 35.4 (Jag_cz); 37.1 (Linda Bucklin); 39.1 (lunamarina); 40.1 (SpeedKingz); 40.3 (ImageFlow); 40.4 (Tyler Olson); 40.5, 57.7, 62.4, 88.9, 94.5, 94.7, 95.2, 97.2, 99.1, 103.2, 114.1 (Monkey Business Images); 40.6 (panuwat phimpha); 40.23 (Firma V); 41.1 (Victoria Allum); 43.1 (Marcel Jancovic); 43.2 (SLP_London); 43.3 (sylv1rob1); 44.1, 64.6, 81.3 (New Africa); 45.1 (Dan76); 46.1 (Chinnapong); 46.2, 87.2, 113.2 (Arthimedes); 48.1 (stockwerk-fotodesign); 48.2 (Reeva); 48.3 (streetflash); 48.4 (Alla Khananashvili); 49.1 (MarcoVector); 54.2 (takayuki); 54.3 (Iurii Kachkovskyi); 55.1 (alexkatkov); 56.1 (Massimo De Candido); 56.2 (Dragon Images); 57.1, 86.1, 100.2 (ESB Professional); 57.2 (Stuart Jenner); 57.3 (UfaBizPhoto); 57.4 (JPC-PROD); 57.5 (Indigo Fish); 57.6 (Martin Allinger); 60.1 (Pixel-Shot); 61.2 (tai11); 62.2 (DGLimages); 62.3 (Jan H Andersen); 62.5 (Suzanne Tucker); 62.6 (VH-studio); 63.1 (Serhii Ostapenko); 63.2 (Wojmac); 63.3, 88.4 (Pressmaster); 64.1 (ANTHONY PAZ); 64.2 (Dima Moroz); 64.3 (Roman Samokhin); 64.4 (Ruslan Kudrin); 64.5 (Angorius); 64.7 (Alaettin YILDIRIM); 64.8 (charl898); 68.1 (Aliaksandr Bukatsich); 68.2 (file404); 68.3 (PKpix); 69.1 (Antonio Guillem); 69.2, 106.2 (Prostock-studio); 69.4 (Brainsil); 69.5 (Motortion Films); 70.1 (eurobanks); 70.2 (Dean Drobot); 70.3 (Martina V); 71.2 (Sylvie Bouchard); 71.3 (Enzo Molinari); 74.1 (Thomas Dutour); 74.2 (BDLook); 74.3 (guruXOX); 74.4 (mbrphoto); 74.5 (pisaphotography); 75.1 (Food Travel Stockforlife); 75.2 (Yibo Wang); 76.1 (Yevgen Kravchenko Lizenzfreie); 76.2 (Visual Generation); 76.3, 114.5 (Gelpi); 77.1 (Yusev); 77.2 (ixpert); 80.1 (KlaraBstock); 80.2 (claudia veja images); 80.3 (PRASANNAPIX); 80.4 (Minerva Studio); 80.5 (LightField Studios); 81.1 (Olena Yakobchuk); 81.4 (TaraPatta); 81.5 (santypan); 81.6 (Dragana Gordic); 81.82 (bernatets photo); 82.1 (Victoria Chudinova); 83.1 (Ermolaev Alexander); 88.1 (Iakov Filimono); 88.2 (sirtravelalot); 88.3 (Romariolen); 88.5 (Kaspars Grinvalds); 88.6 (Jantanee Runpranomkorn); 88.7, 95.1 (Jacek Chabraszewski); 88.7 (Nomad_Soul); 89.2 (owatta); 89.3 (Melica); 91.1 (Tap10); 91.2 (Kyle Lee); 94.1 (Peter Kim); 94.2 (oneinchpunch); 94.3 (Ipatov); 95.3 (Ihor Bulyhin); 96.2 (Shift Drive); 97.1 (DedovStock); 98.1 (all_about_people); 100.1 Avatar_023); 100.3 (hxdbzxy); 101.1 (Svetography); 102.1 (Kristina Kokhanova); 102.2 (Elena Stepanova); 103.3 (ivector); 106.3 (pikselstock); 106.5 (George Rudy); 106.6 (SIHASAKPRACHUM); 106.71 (antoniodiaz); 107.1 (Simone Hogan); 107.2 (Marish); 108.1 (CREATISTA); 109.3 (Chereliss); 112.7 (madpixblue); 114 (Irina Strelnikova); 114.2 (Maridav); 114.3 (Timof); 114.4 (VaLiza); 116.1 (Littlepetra); 116.2 (Andrey_Popov); 118.1 (tristan tan); 120.1 (Artur_Sarkisyan); 121.1 (Skumer); 131 (silverkblackstock); 131.2 (Roxana Gonzalez); various (Om Yos); various (ProStockStudio); various (Undergroundarts.co.uk); various (ahmad agung wijayanto); various (flower travelin'; man); various (mhatzapa); various (monticello); various (tatianasun); various.8 (Air Art); 48, 49, 50, 51, 52 (Val_Iva)